ISLAM, DEMOCRACY AND GOVERNANCE IN THE NORTH AFRICAN COUNTRIES

ISLAM, DEMOCRACY AND GOVERNANCE IN THE NORTH AFRICAN COUNTRIES

◆

The Zero Stage of States

Ahmed Jazouli

iUniverse, Inc.

New York Lincoln Shanghai

ISLAM, DEMOCRACY AND GOVERNANCE IN THE NORTH AFRICAN COUNTRIES
The Zero Stage of States

iUniverse books may be ordered through booksellers or by contacting:

iUniverse
2021 Pine Lake Road, Suite 100
Lincoln, NE 68512
www.iuniverse.com
1-800-Authors (1-800-288-4677)

ISBN-13: 978-0-595-40898-6 (pbk)
ISBN-13: 978-0-595-85261-1 (ebk)
ISBN-10: 0-595-40898-2 (pbk)
ISBN-10: 0-595-85261-0 (ebk)

Printed in the United States of America

Contents

Preface ix

Part I

I. Globalization and Democracy 3

II. Islam and democracy: two "rivals" for a common goal 9

III. North Africa escapes the "nationalist" trap 17

IV. Good Governance and North African Complexities 22

- *A. Governance: A Modern View* *22*
- *B. Good governance in traditional societies* *29*

Part II

V. Political, Economic, and Judicial Systems. 41

- *A. Morocco: Historical Roots, Democratic Will, and Schizophrenic Elites* *43*
   1. Scrutinizing Elections 43
   2: Economy: Institutionalizing Modernity 47
   3: The Judicial System: Longing for Independence 51
- *B. Algeria: Oil and Poverty without Democracy.* *55*
   1. Failure of Democracy 55
   2. Economic System: Chaos of the Public Sector. 62
   3. Judicial System: The Weight of the Uniform 64
- *C. Tunisia: Pluralism of the Unique and the Postponed Democracy* *67*
   1. No Right to True Candidacy to Presidency. 67
   2. Economic System: Controlled Liberalism 70

3. Judicial System: Interference by the state 72

• *D. Libya: A Revolution Without The Revolution* *75*

1. A Populist Democracy 75

2. A Populist Policy led to A Populist Economy. 80

3. The Revolution Alone Represents The "Judicial" System. 82

• *E. Egypt: The Oldest And the Latest Democracy* *85*

1. Roots of Elected Bodies: At last an opposition 85

2. Economy: Out of the Totalitarian System 91

3. Judicial System: Fairness and Strength 93

VI. Human Rights In North African Countries 96

• *INTRODUCTION: The Cultural and the Political Context* *96*

• *A. Sovereignty: No Shade For Violators* *98*

• *B. Women: The Forgotten Half.* *101*

• *C. Civil and Political Rights: Daily Abuse* *104*

1. Morocco: Out of Dark. 104

2. Algeria: The failure of the State 114

3. Tunisia: The Most Protective the Most Abusive 119

4. Libya: The Desert of Individual Rights 123

5. Egypt: Religious Intolerance 127

• *Conclusion: The Main Threats* *136*

Part III

VII. Political Parties Tools For Good Governance 141

• *Introduction.* *141*

• *A. Morocco: Rooted pluralism and lack of professionalism* *143*

• *B. Algeria: The Unprepared Pluralism.* *145*

• *C. Tunisia: The Oppressed Opposition.* *147*

• *D. Libya: The Party is the State.* *148*

• *E. Egypt: Marginalized Opposition* *148*

• *Conclusion: indigenizing Democracy* *150*

VIII. Civil Society: Development, Transparency and
Accountability. 152

Part IV

IX. Conclusion: The Zero Stage of States 159

Bibliography 173

Preface

Any phenomenon conceived in a particular way (conceptualized) in a specific historical condition may be conceived in another period in new terms and from a new perspective, or as I shall say, it may be *re-conceptualized*. At the beginning of the new century, the concept of governance should have a new meaning different than what it has meant since the eighteenth century. Democracy, justice, respect of human rights and development has become deciding and crucially important aspects to governance and force the re-conceptualization of the concept and the main institution that produce its practical meaning, which is the state.

Authoritarianism, unfairness in the administration, injustice, corruption and underdevelopment are not only some phenomena of bad governance; but they are some forms of robbery of the people's sovereignty. The evaluation of the state where we find these aspects should be reviewed. It should not be called a state; it has to be named by another concept.

This research is an attempt to re-conceptualize the state in its practical functions in providing governance to society. There is no absolute state. The practice becomes the identifier of the state itself. In this respect, this book deals with North African Countries' governmental practices and accordingly it concludes by a new identification of the states' levels. The book would have been also entitled "Towards New Forms of Governance in North African Countries" as it intends mainly to deal with the actual facts of governance in those countries and their citizens' hope to establish modern states based on people's sovereignty. Its new forms, such as democracy, independence of justice and transparency, are identifiers of the function and manner of governance itself.

Knowing that the North African countries are in the heart of the world's contemporary issues, this book focuses on the main of them including Islam, democracy and governance.

All these aspects take place in an ever-changing world: that of globalization where borders, censorship and customs become meaningless; where local economies should compete international firms (!!).

PART I

I. Globalization and Democracy

The global economy is undergoing a quick and fundamental change that is reshaping political and social relations around the world including North African Countries (NAC). Does this encourage or hinder the spread of democratic values and practices?

The fundamental dilemma of the world economy is that markets are straining to become global, while the institutions that are required for their effective functioning—legal, social and political—remain largely national. The governments are accountable in their conduct of social and economic policy to the electorate they represent and not to international firms.

Democracy is the most effective guarantor of good governance in both the economic and political spheres. Civil liberties, political freedom and participatory procedures are the best ways to ensure appropriate labor standards, environmental sustainability, and economic stability.

Regimes where democracy is restricted or where there is an authoritarian rule, the economic class cannot express itself freely against the governments' policies, which may be based on the absence of transparency and equity. In non-democratic states corruption is a common practice so as favoritism and unfair economic justice.

From the corporate point of view, democracy is the insurance to investment in any country. An independent justice, a fairly elected parliament, and the accountability of the government and its civil servants are the preconditions for any economic performance.

Globalization is perceived as serving exclusively to open national markets to foreign competition. The North African countries are still hesitant in establishing a totally free market system. The more open economies in North Africa are the Moroccan, the Tunisian and The Egyptian. Also, Algeria signed a partnership agreement like the three previous states with the European Union. These partnership agreements between each of the these countries and the European Union provide the establishment of a free zone between each of the states and the European Union around 2010.

It is difficult to establish free markets without free people. The diversity of products may encourage the diversity of ideas unless the states adopt a hard line in opposing the spread of civil and political rights. The Chinese example proves the opposite, especially that China is not far away from North Africa, but there is much difference between the two cases including that the first has been an absolutist regime since a long date and the second is experiencing an awkward democracy, which north African democratic movements are trying to enforce.

A global economy is not tied to national boundaries. International firms look for wide regions where there are no institutional, geographical or political handicaps. Actually in North African countries, there are all the handicaps to push international investors far from the region. Till 2005, North African markets do not encourage the flow of capitals. The governments are trying to change the situation, but there is still a powerful public sector and states are the main investors like any underdeveloped economy.

The borders between Morocco and Algeria were closed for many years. Where borders are open between the other North African countries, there is exaggerated scrutiny and systemic control. The flow of goods is not free and some times it is totally forbidden. Free flow of goods and capitals should be between North African countries first. Globalization will force states to cooperate in order to create the appropriate field for drawing international investments, which will force states to establish a democratic economic system and this will help to the democratization of the states.

Except Libya, all North African countries are members to the World Bank and the World Trade Organization, which urge their members to implement their recommendations including good governance. NAC's membership to the World Bank and the World Trade Organization added to their partnership agreements with the European Union [and Libya should follow], all this will force NAC to be part of the global economy and the region should be part of the global political system, which is democracy.

Transparency and accountability are the main components of any open economic system. Corruption and unaccountable state's bodies and civil servants cannot attract foreign investments, whose freedom of movement is one of the major aspects of globalization. Only democratic institutions can assure transparency and accountability. Through fair periodic elections, elected bodies have to implement policies that assure the citizens' interests and the promotion of their life conditions.

With globalization, North African economies will be a favorite destination of the European capitals. The low wages, the low taxes and the cheaper acres of land—if compared to the European conditions—are encouraging factors to investment. From North Africa, the European based capitals will keep too near to the European markets.

The prosperity that globalization may bring to NAC will encourage North African governments to be more democratic. But what if they choose to be democratic in the economic field and keep hesitant in civil and political rights? The Tunisian government made this choice, but the opposition is leading a harsh campaign to force the state to implement democracy and they are succeeding, especially that some new political parties are tolerated and many candidates can dispute the state's presidency.

Before going on dealing with globalization and democracy, the overall international economic situation arises many crucial questions that the institutional infrastructure in NAC should be ready to respond to. Some of these questions are the following:

a. Nation states for international economy:

The nation state becomes a traditional institution in the new world founded by globalization that forces national firms to be articulated to the international ones, which creates totally international economic relations within states. Sure, there is no international jurisdiction to which should refer this international economy while acting in nation states where the local laws govern.

So, the economic decision-makers would have to deal with different jurisdictions, different norms and different institutions, which makes new costs and additional burdens to the firms' investment budgets. This should urge states to unify their legislations, but this is the most difficult task for North African states. The differences are enormous, as the identities of states are different, so it will not be easy to unify, at least, investment legislations. Despite this situation, NAC are obliged to strive for the unification of their main economic laws to establish a unified area that may be able to attract foreign investors.

b. Family based economy:

In NAC, there are large economic areas where there is a family based economy. Small farms, traditional manufactories and small businesses are established and managed by families. Under the father or the big brother authority all family members participate in running the family projects. There are no 'outsiders'. Wages are not attributed according to national rates, or sometimes there are no wages at all. All the revenue serves to the families' daily needs. This economy will face the threat of its disappearance, which may create enormous numbers of people looking for new jobs. Aware by the challenge of the overall international economic situation, Morocco, Tunisia and Egypt are trying to promote family based economy towards an institutionalized one. Due to the international financial institutions, including the World Bank, the above-mentioned states had started economic adjustment programs many years ago, but there are limited results. People linked to the family based economy are not fervent defenders of democracy, because they are against all kinds of state's intervention. They are against the rule of law and especially accountability and transparency; they are for the community laws. This economy will not be against globalization only; it will be against democracy also.

c.   Traditional trade unionism and markets rule:

In NAC there is a traditional trade unionism especially in well-established public and private firms. The dismissal of workers as a practice of international firms will be strongly rejected not only by trade unions, but by the political parties as well. The trade unions in NAC are known for their historical struggle against colonialism and the states' policies in the aftermath of independence. Streets' manifestations and hundreds of casualties always follow the small decision like the state's rise of the price of bread by less than one cent. The states should work together with trade unions to try to modernize their work in order to be able to respond to any case according to what it requires. A professional trade unionism based on the fight for humanizing economic relationships is needed, and this requires the promotion of dialogue between the two parts: the owners should be responsive and the workers constructive, with the neutral supervision of the state.

The above-mentioned three levels are only the basic problems that an international investor may face. The southern difficulties are not like the northern ones where NGOs are the main opponent to globalization. In NAC, The civil society is emerging. In the near future, it may be able to mobilize thousands of demonstrators to face the World Bank policies. The opposition may be found anywhere and anyhow.

International firms and all those who look for benefits from globalization, including North African States, should be aware that a democratic legal framework is a pre-condition. And local and international business leaders should understand that well-paid, skilled and cooperative workers can be more productive and profitable than those who are exploited and angry. Human capital accumulates more quickly in democratic societies, and today, human capital is the driving force of development and prosperity.

A human globalization may be an encouraging factor to establish democracy especially in southern states like North African Countries. But democratization is not immanent in or an inevitable result of economic globalization. Democracy will require the political commitment of the leadership, the elite and the population if it is to be achieved. To be successful, democracy should become part of the people's cultural values (*).

(*) See: Dr. Ahmed JAZOULI, "Polls Alone Don't Make a Democracy" in "Global Politician" magazine. Issue 10/15/2005:
http://globalpolitician.com/articledes.asp?ID=1284&cid=2&sid=44

II. Islam and democracy: two "rivals" for a common goal

Most of the Islamic states are not democratic. The better ones are on the way towards democracy. This situation added to some Islamist movements' open resentment to democracy, let most analysts say that democracy is against Islam. In fact, the relation between democracy and Islam is more complex than this (1).

At the beginning of the last century, Islamic countries, except Saudi Arabia, were suffering from colonization. Independence was a concluded arrangement between the colonization authorities and the colonized territories. Independence declarations were not the expression of total independence except for a small number of cases like Algeria, which has got its independence from France after a long and harsh war of liberation. In both cases democracy was not an immediate urgency for the two states. Those who called for democracy were either thrown of government (Benbela in Algeria) or discarded from political arrangements (the Moroccan political party "The Party for Democracy and Independence" lead by Bell-Hassan Al-Ouazzani).

After independence, strengthening national sovereignty and starting economic growth were the fascinating projects for any government hoping for popularity. It was easy to reject any democratic political project just because it hides Western values. Most of the states had established the one-party system, which was an answer to the "Western" political experience.

Democracy has not been considered till it was seen as a mean to keep equilibrium between the rival fractions of the society (Morocco, Jordan, Lebanon, etc....). This approach has lead to false democratic regimes. Pluralism was assured, but without the total freedom of expression and association. The press was muzzled, and there were hundreds of political detainees.

After the crackdown of the Eastern political system and the international influence of human rights movements, with the help of the internal fights for democracy and human rights, most of the Muslim traditional regimes are experiencing transitions towards democratic systems (Morocco, Jordan, etc...). The new regimes that were established in specific conditions had chosen their own "democracy" (e.g. Iran).

Though these developments, the relation between democracy and Islam is still an actual debate rooted in the history of Islam itself. Before all and else, could Islam as a religion be considered a theory of state? Ancient Muslim scholars had elaborated what is called "interpretation" *(Ijtihad)* of the Qu'ran and the prophet's sayings *(Hadith)* to prove that there is an "Islamic theory of state". But I think all we can find in Islam some guidelines that may be understood as theoretical principles for a political system. When we deal with a religion and a political theory, we are dealing with two different and independent fields. The first where the truth is absolute (ordinance of God) and the second where there can be more than one truth; the relative truth of human sciences. The Islamic Holly Book, the Qu'ran, offers a lot of verses about justice and orders that decisions should be taken after consultations were made. But the way to choose the leadership, to make justice and consultation in decision-making was let to the people's decision.

When the prophet Muhammad was dead, he left no recommendation about how to appoint his successor. At the time, the elite of the Muslim society, which was a united state, had to choose the leader of the nation (the Caliph)*. This elite (decision-makers) was composed of the prophet's companions and the nobles of the prophet's tribe named Kuraish. At the beginning, they were divided into two parties: those who wanted the first companion of the prophet Abu Baker Essedik and those who were for one of the nobles from Kuraish. At the end, the choice was made, and Abu Baker was appointed Caliph and another man from Kuraish was appointed *Wazir* (minister) (2).

So, we can deduce that there is no religious ordinance about how to choose the national leader, but it should be a matter and a result of consultation. Also, the Islamic nation was for the representation of the different parts [companions of the prophet and Kuraish] without exclusion.

Before his death, Abu Baker recommended that the Muslims should appoint as Caliph another prophet's companion whose name is 'Omar Ibn Al-Khattab. After Abu Baker's death, the Muslims confirmed his choice. But Ibn Al-Khattab had not named anyone and delegated the matter to six of the prophet's companions who, after his death had chosen Othman Ibn Affan whose murder marked a turning point in Islamic history, when two of the companions of the prophet wanted to be Caliphs: Ali Ibn Abi Taleb and Mouawiya Ibn Abi Soufian. The later defeated the first and declared himself Caliph. Before his death, he had appointed his elder son Yazid hereditary of the Caliphate. From that time, the primogenitor system was established, but it has been a highly controversial question along the Islamic history (3).

Ibn Khaldun (1332–1395) said that "limiting succession within [the Caliph's] children is not of the aims of the religion"(4), but some others, referring to a quotation of Omar Ibn Al-Khattab, say that the recommendations made by him and his predecessors did not exclude the Caliph's relatives including his children, but they all insist that Caliphate should be discerned after consultation with decision-makers and it should not be against the people's will (5).

Ibn Khaldun, Al-Mawardi and many other scholars insist that there should be many conditions for a man to be Caliph (6). For them all, the common condition is that the Caliph should be just. They refer to a verse in the Qu'ran, which says that "if you judge, judge with justice" (7). The prominent scholars Al-Ghazali, al-Shafii and al-Iji went further in assuring the people's right to end the Caliph's reign. Al-Ghazali said: "The unjust Sultan should give up his mandate, or be put aside." Al-Shafii said the "the Imam should be put aside if he is an adulterer or unjust and the same for any judge or governor". Al-Iji recommended "the Umma (the nation) has the right to discard the Imam for any specific reason that requires that."

The same for consultations in all matters related to the state's affairs. From the Caliphate till daily life decisions, Muslim scholars insist on consultation as it is clearly stated by the Qu'ran. In the 159th verse of Surah (chapter) Âl-'Imran it is said that: "They by the Mercy of Allah, you dealt with them gently. And had you been severe and harsh-hearted, they would have broken away from you; so pass over (their faults), and ask (Allah's) Forgiveness for them; and consult them in the affairs. Then when you have taken a decision, put your trust in Allah, certainly, Allah loves those who put their trust (in Him)". Consultation was limited to decision-makers. Al-Mawardi called them "those who choose" and said that those who should belong to this category of the society should fulfill three conditions: (a) To be totally just; (b) highly qualified scholars; and (c) wise (8).

All the above-mentioned views and principles may be considered as seeds for democracy. We can learn that no one has the right to declare himself president of the state, and any statesman should be just and decisions should be taken after consultations. The most important body in the Islamic traditional state was that of "decision makers" (*those who tie; those who loose*) and there is no clear reference to people or citizens as it is the case for modern democracies.

Abdelwahhab Al-Affendi says that: "In the early periods of Islam, the 'Muslim' and 'citizen' were identical concepts." He replies to Bernard Lewes who says that the absence of the word 'citizen' from the Arab language was because of the lack of citizen's participation. Al-Affendi adds that at the beginning of the Islamic society every Muslim had the right to participate in decisions. He called this "an active citizenship". He argued that 'Muslim' and 'citizen' were identical because of people used to belong automatically to the land where they are. Based on a prophet's saying, Al-Affendi emphasized that women and freed slaves had also the right to take decisions in the mosque, which was during the prophet's days the office of government where believers gather for prayers and discussions. Al-Affendi insisted that till modern days citizenship is related to the individual's link as a member of the local community where he lives". He confirmed that the International Covenant on Civil and Political Rights provides the same thing (9).

In Islam, the Imam should hear from everyone, as it is the case for the priest in Christianity, though the Imam has both the religious and the political authority and not like the priest. Also, it is an obligation for the Imam to act according to the nation's consensus. The Prophet said: "My nation does not consent upon something wrong." This is the main principle in any democracy. It reflects the people's sovereignty.

Though these affirmations, whether Islam tolerates democracy as it is practiced by the western states is still an active debate in Islamic countries. Since the days of their Father Founders like Hassan Al-Bena and Sayed Kotb, Islamist movements used to say that consultation is sufficient in Muslim states. They say that it should be within Muslim theologian who should be the decision-makers.

Longing to get power, the first Islamists tried to convince head of states to rally their movements. In Sudan, the Islamist movement lead by Hassan Turaby succeeded with Jaâfar Numeiri who is an ex-president of the state. He was socialist and turned to an Islamist who had implemented Sharia law at the beginning of the 1980s. He is known for his famous mutilations for petty thefts. The Islamist movement in Egypt tired to do the same with Anouar Sadat. When he refused, they killed him in1981.

When the Islamists failed in many other countries to make change through alliance with autocratic heads of states, they turned towards the peoples to make revolutions, and those who failed; they tried to experience elections as a mean to take the power.

Democracy is more than elections. It is a cultural value and a practice of the state's policy based on human rights and the rule of law. UN Resolution 1999/57 affirmed that democratic governance includes, inter alia, the following: a) the right to freedom of expression, association and believe; b) the rule of law, fairness in the administration of justice and independence of the judiciary; c) the right of citizens to choose their governmental system through constitutional or other democratic means; d) the right of political participation, including equal opportunity for citizens to become candidates; and d) transparent and accountable government institutions.

In Iran, the Islamist movement could get power after a popular revolution in 1979. The first authority in the country is that of the Guide of the

Revolution called *"Al-Murshid"*. The Muslim highly qualified theologists elect him. With the Guide, they constitute the religious authority, which approves the candidacy to the presidential elections. Once successful by vote, the president should be approved by the *"Al-Murshid"*(10). Though non-Muslims vote, there is no political party that does not belong to the religious system in place. More than this, Iran's human rights' records are very bad and civil and political rights suffer a lot.

In Algeria, the Islamist movement lead by Abassi Madani called the "Islamic Salvation Front" (FIS) participated in 1992 two tour parliamentary elections, which gave it the majority. The government refused to hold the second tour, stopped the whole process and banned the FIS. The government based its reaction on the fact that Islamists wanted to use elections to ban democracy. It had advanced a declaration of the second man in the FIS Ali Belhaj, who had said: "For us, democracy is just a tactic."

Most of the Arab constitutions provide that Islam is the religion of state. But there are only three states where the head of the state has religious authorities: Morocco, Jordan and Saudi Arabia. In Morocco and Jordan there is an emergent democracy and people can partly change their government through elections, but Saudi Arabia has just experienced elections at the local level. The king of Morocco Mohammed VI said openly that: "There is no contradiction between human rights and Islam." According to the constitution, he is the Commander of Believers (*Emir Almouminin*), but he appoints the Prime Minister, who has to go to the House of Representatives in the parliament to look for support. If he gets the majority by vote, he takes office.

The Arab countries with the presidential systems would have been more democratic. But after their independence they established socialist regimes with the one-party system. Though they introduced the multi-party laws, the structure of the ancient one-party is still hegemonic although it had changed its name and its ideology. In these countries, the opposition says that elections are still unfair. So, democracy is still too far to be reached. The regimes' reluctance to establish democratic political systems is due to the hegemonic lobbies' refusal and the weakness of democracy supporters, and the situation has nothing to do with Islam itself.

Islamist movements made of Islam a political theory of state. I think that any Muslim can find in this religion some guidelines to what he thinks about, but not a complete theory. The evolution made that the concept of the state itself is changing continuously and methods of governance are in an on-going revolution. Using Islam as a theory of state needs a coming back to the texts of the Qu'ran and the *Hadith*. As they are so many aspects of life that were not during the prophet's reign, decision-makers should interpret the Qu'ran and the *Hadith*. And as interpretation is a human behavior and we may have many interpretations to the same phenomenon, why some movements are still hiding behind Islam to express their own views. Sure, they want their positions to be above any criticism. So, I think that decision-makers should decide freely and there should be a democratic regime to make them accountable.

Not only some Islamists movements, but also all those who are against democracy hide behind the veil that they are against the West. In modern days democracy became universal and consultation and justice in Islam and other religions may be considered the essence of any democracy.

Democracy is forcing its way and those who oppose it, however their identity is, are considered by people as if they want to escape accountability and wish to go on protecting their own interests against their peoples' will.

Also, being for or against any political system is a political position, not a religious one. The case of terrorism is the most obvious example. Terrorism as a way to "lead the struggle against the West" has nothing to do with Islam. It's the theory of the hopeless who think that the peaceful defense of any cause is aimless. Muslims are hopeful or they should be so according to religion itself. If engaged in any fight, religion should urge people to put dialogue ahead. To make change, Muslim activists should convince the majority through lobbying and put the international public opinion to their side. Instead of financing the industry of suicide bombers, they have to invest in media, civil society and decision makers all over the world.

The main peaceful fight should be within Islamic states instead of being at the international level. When Muslims in their home countries will enforce fairly elected governments that respect the universal values of human rights, their states will not be underestimated and their defense for the right cause will be heard.

Islam is a religion, but democracy is a system of government. Every field has its own components and goals and both of them should enhance the values of freedom, dialogue and justice. But when the Islamic traditional texts became laws, they start to be against the rule of law, against democracy and human values.

---

(1) John L.Esposito and John O. Voll. Islam and Democracy. In http://www.neh.fed.us/news/humanities/2001-11/islam.html

See also, Ali R. Abootaleb. Islam, Islamists, And Democracy. In Middle East Review of International Affairs (MERIA). Volume3, No.1—March 1999. in http://www.biu.ac.il/SOC/besa/meria/journal/1999/issue1/jv3n1a2.html

(*) The Caliph, the Imam and Emir Almouminin mean the same.

(2) Alfred Guillaume. Penguin Books, Great Britain. Second edition 1956 reprinted in 1982.

(3) W. Muir. The Caliphate, its Rise, Decline, and Fall. Edinburgh, 1924.

(4) Cited in: Doctor Mohammed Dasser. Political Thoughts in Islam. [In Arabic]. First Edition, Rabat (without date).

(5) Ibid.

(6) See: Abd Al-Rahman Ibn Khaldun. "Muqadima" (Prolegomena) [In Arabic], and Abdu'l-Hassan al-Mawardi. "Al-Ahkam As-Sultaniyyah" (The Laws of Islamic Governance) [in Arabic]. First Edition. Assaâada Print, Cairo, 1909.

(7) The Qu'ran. Surah 5 Al-Mâida: 42.

(8) Doctor Said Bensaid. "Theology and Politics" [In Arabic]. First Edition, Dar Alhadatha, Beirut, 1987.

(9) Abdelwahhab Al-Affendi. Reviewing the Traditional Concept to the Political Community in Islam: A Muslim or a Citizen?" in Al-Mustaqbal Al-Arabi. No. 264, February 2001.

(10) The Constitution. Iran.

III. North Africa escapes the "nationalist" trap

Pan—Arab nationalism had influenced political developments in North African Countries (NAC). It was at the origin of the creation of many political movements and both Gamal Abdul Nasser and Mouamar Kadhafi consider themselves those who had implemented the Pan—Arab ideology after they got power in 1954 and 1968 respectively. In Morocco, Algeria and Tunisia Pan—Arab nationalism was limited to marginal political parties, but the books of the Father Founders were widely read and their writers were considered national leaders.

Democracy was not of the interests of the Pan—Arab nationalists. Their main aims were: a) strengthening the Arab peoples feeling of their identity after centuries of the Othmans' occupation and decades of colonization; b) building a united Arab state from Morocco to Iraq and from Syria to Yemen; and c) the hopped for state should be an economically developed country based on equality and justice (1).

The most used concept in the Pan—Arab writings is 'The Nation' (*Al-Umma*). The Individual was seen as an opposite to the community as a whole. The German unification under Bismarck was given as an example. Some gave also the example of Hitler. Others went further and had founded an identical party to that of Hitler and they called it "The National Socialist Arab Party". The British and the French experiences were discarded because the two states were seen as enemies. The principle of citizenship that is based on the individual was looked at as something that would hinder the national unity (2).

Satiâ Al-Hasri asked the question "who we are?" His answer was the identity built on language first. Some hints that may be considered related to citizenship are found in Munif Arazzaz writings when he speaks about the relation between the individual and the state. In 1952, he said that there are political, economic and civil rights. He considers them some aspects of the modern life (3).

Yassine Al-Hafid who is one of the famous Pan—Arab nationalists titled one of his books "The Nationalist Question and Democracy", but he dedicated it to his reply to those "who had lost trust in Pan—Arab nationalism" including those who struggle for democracy (4).

Pan—Arab nationalism founders were not interested in democracy. Those who went beyond the nation's unity as a general idea, called for socialism. The two main Pan—Arab political parties that were founded were socialists: The Baâth Party (in Syria and Iraq) and The Movement of the Arab Nationalists (in Lebanon, Yemen and other Arab countries). The last movement started to approach democracy, when it was convinced that socialism could not be realized in the Arab countries before transforming the economy into its capitalist's form. This was at the end of the 1960s and the early 1970s (5).

The struggle for democracy is a modern aspect of the Arab political movement interests. In the past, democracy was considered just a step towards socialism, but not a goal. Pan—Arab theorists were saying that socialism could not be applied in an underdeveloped social situation where there is no workers class. So, they thought that the first thing to do was to struggle for the creation of a national authority lead by the national capitalists who were supposed able to establish democracy in its western form. According to the same movement, these capitalists would be able to create the workers' class, which should have been the leader of the socialist revolution against the capitalists. It was supposed that capitalists would be Pan-Arabs allies against landowners, but these landowners were those who had turned to capitalist investors, as the Arab countries had not undergone any industrial revolution like Europe. Landowners cooperated with the western capitalists and turned the Arabs consumers of the western goods. Instead of developing a capitalist class based on production factories, the Arab societies gave birth to a rich merchant class who had erected strong firms specialized in import. Unfortunately there was no workers class and even a capitalist one like what is in the western countries. So, democracy was still looking for a social defender.

Pan—Arab nationalists were supposing that liberals should be their allies to defend democracy, but neither liberals nor communists were convinced of this theory. The firsts considered them opportunists and the seconds considered them at the beginning utopians before adopting the same position like liberals in a later time.

What is most important in this theory is that most Pan—Arab intellectuals started to promote democracy. Some of them went further and considered themselves convinced of democracy especially after the crackdown of the Soviet Union and the end of socialism. These are the modern Pan—Arab nationalists who had founded the "Pan—Arab Congress" in 1999. This movement's dedication to democracy is obvious. Its founding declaration says that: "The rebirth of the Arab nation would not be acquired without achieving it in every country. This will not be done unless democracy and human rights are promoted, the individual rights respected and the relation between the individual and the state established on the rule of law" (6).

To the Pan—Arab nationalist this position reflects a split between the modern and the old view that was preaching for a large and united Arab state and which considers those who call for democracy acting against union and encouraging contradictions within the Arab society.

Some of the Father Founders of the "Pan—Arab Congress" are Borhan Ghalyoun, Mohammed Abed El-Jabri and Abdul—Illah Bellakziz. The last one, who is a Moroccan writer, had started his activities as a Marxist—Leninist and was converted to a Pan—Arab nationalist, before adding democracy and calls for dialogue with Islamists to his cultural struggle. He emphasized this idea of democracy in one of his recent books when he wrote that: "separating the struggle for democracy from the struggle for the Arab unity was one of the reasons for the failure of the project for the Pan—Arab national unity" (7). Mohamed Abed El-Jabri and Borhan Ghalyoun were the first scholars who paved the way for human rights and democracy within the Arab "nationalist" community.

The Pan—Arab movement did not start to be an ardent advocate of democracy till it has been a popular demand for all social classes in the Arab States. This opportunism within the Pan—Arab movement appears also through its longing for dialogue with the Islamist movement. In the past, they were fervent enemies. Islamists were calling for the Muslim countries unity and Pan—Arab nationalists were hoping for a limited unity to Arab states. For the first, identity was based on language, but for the others it was based on religion. How they concluded their union in the "Pan—Arab Congress" is still an enigma, unless every party wants to use the other one to restore or develop its popularity.

The choice of the Islamist movements as an ally made an end to the secularist tendencies within the Pan—Arab movement. At its beginning, most of its founders were secular intellectuals. They were hoping for the establishment of a modern Arab state based on the positive law, while Islamist movements were preaching for the implementation of the Islamic law. Positive law and secularism do not exclude despotism, but some modern Arab human rights activists say that if the secular tendencies were encouraged within the early Pan—Arab movements, there would have been more opportunities for democracy.

The Syrian, Iraqi and the Libyan governments were calling themselves Pan—Arab nationalists. These states' records in the fields of democracy and human rights were dark. The opposition was outlawed, there are hundreds of political detainees and the press was under the state's control.

As it was mentioned before, the Pan—Arab nationalism had not turned to an advocate of democracy till the recent years with the "Pan—Arab Congress." This change may be temporary because of this movement crisis, as it became an elitist movement with no popular support and its idea of establishing a united Arab state became old fashioned since the Arab states had established their own political identity.

Also, democracy is a modern interest of the Arab peoples and not only the Pan—Arab nationalists. After independence, some of the political movements, which were calling for democracy, did so just because they wanted themselves to be in power, but that was not a conviction. Their main aims were economic independence from the West, education for all and building a strong infrastructure. Some others called for industrialization.

With human rights movements, democracy started to be an effective interest of the Arab societies. Knowing that most of the Arab states had ratified the International Covenant on Civil and Political Rights, which provides that all citizens have the right to "take part in the conduct of public affairs", human rights activists launched many campaigns for democracy. Some Pan—Arab ideologists did not welcome this because human rights activists were calling for democracy as a whole towards the states and towards movements including the Pan—Arab ones. The Pan—Arab movement strengthened the feeling of the Arab identity, encouraged learning the Arab language through education, but it cannot be considered one of the main fighters for democracy in the Arab countries.

---

(1) Satiâ Al-Hasri. "Arabism First" (in Arabic). Dar Al-Ilm Lilmalayin, Beirut, 1955.

(2) Abdullah Rimawi. "The Pan-Arab Revolutionary Declaration", the Second Edition. Cairo, the Egypt Resurrection Library, 1966.

(3) Munif Arazzaz. Aspects of the New Arab Life", the First edition. Cairo, 1952.

(4) Yassine Al-Hafid. "The Nationalist Question And Democracy". Bierut, 1980.

(5) Mahdi Amil. "In Contradiction", Beirut, 1982.

(6) The Pan-Arab Congress and the Center for Arab Unity Studies. "The Situation of the Arab Nation: The second Pan-Arab Conference—Documents—Decisions—Declarations". Beirut, March 1999.

(7) Abdul-Illah Bellakziz. "Nationalism and Secularism: Ideology and History". Dar Alkalam. Rabat, 1989.

IV. Good Governance and North African Complexities

A. GOVERNANCE: A MODERN VIEW

After the presidential elections in Somalia on August 31, 2000, the New York Times entitled its report: "Somalis Get leader, now they need a Nation." (1) This raised the question: What is a nation? This term is often used by some political theorists to mean any "sovereign state with political autonomy and settled territory" (2). Others say "nation" refers rather to "the population within a territory, sharing a common culture, language, and ethnicity with a strong historical continuity. This manifests itself in most members in a sentiment of collective, communal identity" (3). But as the reference is made to Somalia where the civil war ravaged every thing, how do citizens experience their identity? For people of that country and many other States where there is no democracy and human rights are not respected, a nation may mean more than that. Wherever we find sovereign people we may say that there is a nation. And to be sovereign means also to participate in decision-making.

Before all and else, governance is to be practiced in a well-established state. The age of theories has vanished. Actually, it is the age of facts (4). In the 19th century, force was the main mean to keep power. Kings were either brave battle leaders or they would lose their crowns. Inside or outside their countries, sword in hand, they were ready to kill every opponent. Monarchs who earned and maintained their people's love, or consider what they say, were scarce.

Throughout history, scholars were interested in different facets of power. They explained its evolution, analyzed its dimensions in theory and practice, and proposed how power should be exercised "better", and the countries' great historical events gave scholars great opportunities to create new theories.

In Italy, wars between Principalities one time, and their union another time were both incitements to new thoughts, if not new theories and theorists that are still influencing most of world leaders. One of these is Nicola Machiavelli (1469–1527) and his theory. For him, "a prince should have other goal, other things to think about, other arts, more than war and preparing it. It is the suitable art of the leader" (5). And "if he wants to preserve his throne, he has to learn to be wicked, and resort to this art, or not, as circumstances require"(6). In a question and answer play, he wrote: "Is it better to be loved than feared, or feared than loved?" Then, Machiavelli answered himself: "both are necessary, but as it is difficult to handle them together, the safest is to be feared than loved, especially when there is the obligation to drop one of them"(7). His main goal while giving his "precious advice" to monarchs is that the monarch (The Prince) should keep power.

Machiavelli's famous book "The Prince" is for the most part a long answer to the short question: How to preserve the throne? Also, when he talks about the need of institutions—like parliament—it is just to let monarchs "put on other's back unpleasant works and save good ones to themselves" (8). This immorality "should" be "reflected in the positions of the prince" (9).

Without drawing any distinction between what's right and what's wrong, Machiavelli suggests that a prince can never be neutral; he has either to be for or against. "A prince is respected when his friendship or unfriendly relations are not doubtful; that is to say when he declares himself frankly for or against someone. Taking position is always profitable than remaining neutral"(10). For Machiavelli, the notion of "justice" or what is called actually "public interest" as a goal for practicing power doesn't exist at all. He is the author of the famous maxim: "The end justifies the means"(11).

In France, for many political theorists, the Constitution of 1789 was a result and a catalyst of new political theories. It was for them an occasion to put forward their ideas, and many of them were invited by monarchs to participate in discussions.

I chose a famous essay that was referred to by many scholars; it is an "Essay about Human, Citizen, and Nation's rights; or Message to the King about Estates General and Principles of a Good Constitution," written by Jean-Louis Seconds (12). For Seconds, "the art of governing people is the art of making them happy"(13). In opposition to what Machiavelli wrote in "The Prince", Seconds says, "obedience shouldn't be based on fear, but on the need of order and duty spirit." He adds: "Freedom shouldn't be a favor; it is just in itself the most sacred and inviolable of all rights" (14). What makes the difference between Machiavelli and Seconds is that the later considers law as "the Queen of GODS and human being (…) Law should be like death; it does not spare anyone" (15).

The author's emphasis on law doesn't make him forget the head of State: "Hundred thousands without a chief aren't more than zeros without unity."(16) This means that Seconds' looking for freedom doesn't make him forget the need for leadership represented by the King. He thought that people and Kings have the same goals: "These principles that we lay down are for the happiness of people and Kings," he emphasized (17). These theories of the 16th, 17th, and 18th centuries influenced many world leaders, but The Prince was taken most of times as the unique reference, which led to despotism and dictatorship in many countries.

Societies have been developing continuously. And "*shared power systems*" (18) were established nearly all over the world. Elections meant that changing governments is not more than a matter of proceedings. In presidential systems or monarchical ones, the level of electoral influence on choosing cabinets has started to become obvious. Developments made that monarchs are capable of reigning without ruling (19), but other countries' developments made some self appointed presidents govern for life, and cover their usurpation of power by unfair elections and on-going oppression (20).

Modern international law theorists look for democracy as one of the basic rights that the UN should try to promote and implement. By emphasizing this, they consider that "the right to political participation

(...) for its individual enjoyment is inseparable from its collective effect" (21). The individual's right to political participation is to have the collective right to oust a political leadership. Article 21 of the Universal Declaration of Human Rights guarantees that the "will of the people shall be the basis of the authority of government; [and] this will shall be expressed in periodic and genuine elections which shall be by universal and equal suffrage and shall be held by secret vote or by equivalent free voting procedures" (22).

During the course of their evolution, societies developed their own political, civil, social, and economic organizations that made of public affairs a wide field of action. These organizations want to share power either by a clear participation in parliamentary and presidential elections, or through influence by public opinion.

Although the problems are common to countries all over the world and huge gapes make one experience different from the other, some states think openly about their problems and face them, but others, unfortunately, try to hide them.

In fact, there is no international *"method"* about *"how to govern"*, nor a handbook about *"Governance: Theory and Practice"*, but some leaders developed their own experiences and methods in appeasing most difficult problems. The most successful are those who were able to create a modern state based on the rule of law. Georges Burdeau, a modern scholar, who consecrated a whole book to "The State", wrote that the State "gave an unprecedented form of Power by removing it from men who practice it, to incarnate it in institutions"(23).

International organizations; especially those that work in the field of human rights (NGOs and IGOs) say explicitly that a modern state is where we find a "democratic rule" and insist on the citizens' free participation in choosing their government or political system as an elementary right.

The International Covenant on Civil and political Rights (adopted by the United Nations on December16th, 1966, and entered into force on

March 23rd, 1976) emphasizes that" Every citizen shall have the right and the opportunity, (…) and without unreasonable restrictions:

1. To take part in the conduct of public affairs, directly or through freely chosen representatives;

2. To vote and be elected at genuine periodic elections which shall be by universal and equal suffrage and shall be held by secret ballot; guaranteeing the free expression of the will of elections;

3. To have access, on general terms of equality, to public service in his country"(24).

The same covenant in the following article (25) adds that "all persons are equal before the law and are entitled without any discrimination of the equal protection of the law"(25).

The United Nations' commission of Civil and Political rights called the Committee of Human Rights—while discussing State's periodical reports about the measures they adopt to give effect to the rights recognized in the covenant asked States Parties questions about the implementation of the above mentioned rights including questions about democracy and the rule of law. Although there is the growing influence of international NGOs all over the world as a means to urge countries to be more democratic, Sates aren't accountable in their domestic practices only in front of human rights committees of the United Nations, basically through states' reports (26).

In more than ten years, UNDP has developed a very interesting project called "Good Governance". In its conceptualizing of governance, the UNDP identifies four types that constitute the formal institutional and organizational structure of authoritative decision-making in a modern state:

1. *Economic governance* includes processes of decision making that directly or indirectly affect a country's economic activities or its relationships with other economies. Economic governance has a major influence on social issues, such as equity, poverty and quality of life.

2. *Political governance* refers to decision-making and policy implementation of a legitimate and authoritative state. The state should consist of separate legislative, executive and judicial branches, represent the interests of a pluralist policy, and allow citizens to freely elect their representatives.

3. *Administrative Governance* is a system of policy implementation carried out through an efficient, independent, accountable and open public sector.

4. *Systemic governance* encompasses the processes and structures of society that guide political and social economic relations to protect cultural and religious beliefs and values, and to create and maintain an environment of health, freedom, security and with the opportunity to exercise personal capabilities that lead to a better life for all people (27).

Stability, security, and sustainable development are major aims of good governance. And this cannot be done without a multiparty system where civil society, human rights, and freedom of expression are protected by the legal system.

For this purpose, UNDP developed in 1997 eight characteristics of good governance. It had emphasized that the institutions of governance in the three domains (state, civil society and the private sector) must be designed to contribute to sustainable human development by establishing the political, legal, economic and social circumstances for poverty reduction, job creation, environmental protection and the advancement of women. Much has been written about the characteristics of efficient government, successful businesses and effective civil society organizations, but the eight (8) main characteristics of good governance include: participation, the rule of law, transparency, responsiveness and consensus orientation, equity, effectiveness and efficiency, accountability, and a strategic vision.

Civicus, an international NGO founded in 1994, explains that" the meaning of governance is complex. It is more than multiparty elections, a judiciary, and a parliament. Good governance implies the following:

1. Universal protection of human rights;

2. Laws that are implemented in a nondiscriminatory manner;

3. An efficient, impartial, and quick judicial system;

4. Transparent public agencies and official decision making;

5. Accountability for decision made about public issues and resources by public officials;

6. Devolution of resources and decision-making power to local levels and bodies in rural and urban areas; (and)

7. Participation and including all citizens in debating public policies and choices (28).

The same organization says that "the universal dream of responsive democratic governance in the new millennium" is a political system where citizens are "listened to and invited to participate on issues of public concern and policy on an ongoing basis. Citizens are equating responsive governance not only with formal institutions or systems of democracy but also with the processes and culture of democratic inclusiveness and participatory governance"(29). The legitimate power should be democratic.

Before, Montesquieu (1689–1755) wrote: "The political virtue is a self denial, which is always a very hard thing. We can define this virtue by loving the laws and the country (…). This love is singularly assigned to democracies. In these democracies alone, government is to be put between every citizen's hands, because the government is like everything in the world; to preserve it you have to love it" (30).

Today, many theorists and practitioners of power go further in discussing the subject. They create the concept of empowerment of institutions and citizens. Some go beyond the economic approach based on development. Furthermore, they include enjoyment of rights as the main aspect that leads vulnerable populations to make institutional influence on policies. For the fight against poverty, human rights dimension is determinant. Citizens who are aware of their dignity, they may not accept to live in poor conditions. When people act as citizens with full rights, they are ready to assume their obligations

So, how all the above mentioned aspects are reflected in political systems of the North African countries?

B. GOOD GOVERNANCE IN TRADITIONAL SOCIETIES

The citizens in NAC have the habit to act according to local values and traditions. With high rates of illiteracy and the weakness of the state of law, official rules are not an easy reference for the majority of people especially outside the big cities.

In these countries (31), where many rebellions and coup attempts took place, it seems that the process of governing till recent decades was meant to keep the rulers in power. But actually many things had changed. In old days, the opposition was looked at as a future usurper of power. The aim of Kings and presidents was "to be in power or not to be." After decades of harsh conflicts, most of the countries in North Africa at the beginning of the new millennium were either cooperating or in a dialogue with their opposition. Though very long, discussions are going on, and the region is in an advanced stage. Although people are still enduring many difficulties and governments use violence and arbitrary arrest towards the opposition, there is no little chance to return to the old practices.

Facing economic, political, religious and ethnic issues is the main burden. Every country tries in its own manner to reform its system of government by solving crucial problems, minimizing risks and developing potentialities. Economic and social problems weigh heavily, and political ones are heavier.

Mohamed VI (King of Morocco) launched a project to re-conceptualize governance as a whole (32). He declared clearly that authorities have to serve people. This happens in a country where citizens (called subjects)

were supposed to serve authorities. He insists on strengthening civil society that is considered as a "bastard" in many third world countries. Also, he made of the struggle against poverty, implementing the rule of law, promoting human rights, and declaring war on illiteracy, some of his main goals. The Moroccan traditional opposition was in power since March 17th, 1998. Appointed by Mohamed VI's predecessor King Hassan II, the Prime minister, Mr. Abderrahman Alyoussoufi (leader of the Socialist Union of Popular Forces—USFP) formed his government by the help of six Parties that formed the opposition: National Rally of Independents (RNI), Istiklal Party (PI), National Popular Movement (MNP), Democratic Forces Front (FFD), and Democratic Socialist Party (PSD).

The arrival of the opposition to government in 1998 was a unique experience in Arab countries. This was made peacefully and after parliamentary election results were known. When the USFP won, the King Hassan II called its leader to form a new cabinet (33).

Though Morocco organized in September 2002 the best parliamentary elections in its history, this experience went backward when Driss Jettou (Independent) was appointed Prime Minister. When he formed his cabinet, the ex-opposition went on in power. The Islamic moderate movement Development and Justice Party (PJD) led the opposition. Also, the "Justice and Charity Association" (radical islamist) organized several demonstrations all over the country, leading a harsh opposition against the government, political parties and civil society (34). In 2005, Nadia Yassin a prominent woman in this movement called for a republic in Morocco, but her call made no echoes.

Algeria, after years of civil war characterized by atrocious slaughters (30), Abdelaziz Bouteflika was elected President on April 28th, 1999. He was minister of foreign affairs during Houary Boumedien's mandate. Boumedien was the first president of the socialist Algeria who led a successful coup attempt in 1964, against Ahmed Benbela the first president after independence from France in 1962 (35).

Bouteflika's main goal was to bring peace to his country. He declared a reconciliation program based on amnesty for rebels who accept to surrender their arms. He was hoping that this solution could stop the Islamists' revenge. In December 1991, the first round of parliamentary elections gave the Islamic Salvation Front (FIS) success. The army generals forced the resignation of President Chadli Benjdid, abolished elections, and presidency was assumed by a collegial presidency lead by the General Khalid Nezar. Shortly after, the collegial presidency named Boudiaf president of the republic without general elections. When he launched a campaign against corruption, he was killed mysteriously (36).

Successively appointed presidents were unsuccessful (37). They couldn't bring stability to the country. Already appointed president, Lyamin Zeroual organized presidential elections that made him the legal president of Algeria. Civil war destroyed the country. Thousands of casualties that international sources have estimated between 100.000 and 150.000 persons were civilians and soldiers and police officers from the lower ranks in the army and the police force. Army wing of the FIS called the Islamic Salvation Army (AIS) was able to kill high officials. Whole families were executed. Terror was all over the country.

A plan to bring peace declared by Bouteflika succeeded at the beginning. In January 2000, AIS dissolved itself, but some extremist fractions continued their war. Though the general amnesty was proposed to the people through a referendum in 2005, news about murder were heard nearly every day (38).

This situation put off any serious thought and discussion about other political problems. Once a candidate for presidential elections was considered as the candidate of the army, the other main candidates, in presidential elections, withdraw on the eve of the Election Day. When elected, he didn't open dialogue with the opposition. The FIS is still outlawed, and its two leaders were denied their freedom of movement for many years. Abassi Madani spent many years under house arrest before traveling to the gulf where he is taking refuge, and Ali Belhaj who was released to be kept under house arrest was returned to prison in July 2005 for praising a terrorist act before being released again (39).

Civil society is emerging and there are some signs of future wake after years of totalitarian rule. As security is always threatened, the importance of other political and economic issues is nearly out of interest.

When the conflict between the president and Generals of the Popular National Army was echoed in the press in 2000 and 2001, new killings took place, and poor farmers were slaughtered in their homes like sheep. Habib Souadia, an ex-army officer, published a testimony book (40) blaming the army of being behind killings in Algeria saying that he was personally ordered to kill civilians when he was in the army.

In Tunisia, President Zinalabidin Benali is trying to build a liberal economy without political liberalism (41). It is based on services economy, which is the highest in North Africa, with 60 per cent of GDP, and 3 millions of labor forces (42). Tunisian government is formed by the president's party Constitutional Democratic Party (PDC), which governs the country since 1963 (8th Jan) although it had changed names since it was founded by ex-president Habib Bourguiba (1957(25th July)–1987 (7th Nov) under the banner of the New Constitutional Party (43).

Democracy is far of being achieved. The opposition is outlawed, and the government itself encouraged a formal one. The Islamist movement "Annahda" was banned, and the secular party Socialist Democratic Movement (MDS) also. Rachid Ghanouchi, leader of "Annahda", is living in exile, and Mohamed Mouaâda of the second is living under house arrest. International human rights organizations considered Tunisia (in 2000) the state that violated the most its citizens' rights (44).

Human rights reports said that Habib Ellouz, a former leader of "Annahda" was life sentenced by a military tribunal in 1992. When he began a hunger strike in 2004, he was transferred. Security forces allegedly used violence against opposition activists and journalists. Nabil Elouaer, whom a military tribunal sentenced to 15 years in the 1990s, was beaten by the head of borj Erroumi prison and put in solitary confinement, where four other prisoners raped him in June 2004. Knowing about this fact, Benali ordered an investigation. Though these human rights records, Ghanouchi enjoyed from the international atmosphere that encourage democracy in MENA countries, and called for dialogue with the government in 2005.

On October 24th, 2004 president Benali was re-elected to serve for a fourth term of 5 years. Though three candidates run against him, he received 94.48 per cent of votes.

In Libya, the most important development in the recent years was lifting the economic embargo imposed by the UN. Many western governments reestablished direct diplomatic relations with Libya since June 2004. Though its new declared will for openness, the rich totalitarian regime with an economy based on consuming the income of oil sells, gave no opportunity to NGO nets and political opposition, and went to harsh oppression of their activists.

A Pan Am plane crashed over Lockerbie in 1988. Two Libyans were considered suspects. Libya refused to hand them over to be prosecuted either in USA or in Britain. After years of suffering, Libya agreed that they should be tried in a neutral state. In 1999, the UN left sanctions endured by Libyan economy since 1992. UN sanctions were left, but Colonel Mouamar Kadhafi is still looked at as a supporter of terrorism and army conflicts. This is an image he has been trying to cast off. His go-between to solve the Irish problem, or to free hostages in the Philippines, confirmed—instead—his relations with what the west called international terrorism. Kadhafi considered most extremist organizations as liberation movements. He supported them by offering arms, training, and secret service help (45). He enjoyed the situation of cold war. When bi-polarity international system crashed, Kadhafi considered himself to be the most appropriate to participate in solving international and regional army crises. While it was hoped by Libyans that this offer might really help in doing much to bring solutions to the most complicated problems, western countries considered it a proof of his links with terrorist groups.

After Saddam Hussein's crack down, Kaddafi declared himself ready to ban his programs to produce weapons of mass destruction. This had opened the way for lifting the embargo, but there were no signs that the regime will leave the totalitarian rule.

In Egypt, the regime is based on a liberal economy and a limited pluralism in politics (46). Democracy is far of being reached. Since 1981, Husni Mubarak was following an economy based on openness against an old state economy that was built by president Gamal Abdul Nasser (1954–1970). When Anouar Sadat (1970–1981) succeeded him, he went on for some years on the same path, but in the mid 1970s he started to free economy, and political pluralism was founded in 1976. With its new constitution in 1971, Egypt not only buried Nasser's domestic policy, but his foreign one as well. In 1978, a peace agreement was signed with Israel. Three years after, an Islamist extremist killed Sadat who signed it, and Islamic political extremism started to spread within different social classes, which draw Egypt to a period of statelessness.

The Egyptian president Mubarak leads a policy based on facing extremism and promoting private sector without encouraging the civil society and democracy (47). Today, a wide range of political parties form the opposition. In 2005, Egypt buried the unique candidate to state presidency that was a fact protected by a law mechanism. Parliament (The Peoples Assembly) used to nominate the president who was confirmed four times by popular referendum (48).

In 2005 demonstrations erupted in streets calling for pluralistic presidential elections. Under pressure, Mubarak proposed amendment of article 76 of the constitution. On May 25th, 2005 the referendum opened up Egypt's presidential elections to opposition candidates after months of debates and popular demonstrations. The opposition led by the Popular Egyptian Movement for Change (known as "Kifaya" which means enough) calls for Mubarak withdrawal from presidency after ending his fourth term. On July 28th, 2005 President Mubarak, 76 years, declared himself candidate for the fifth term!

On September 7th, 2005 Mubarak won the first contested elections, but by the same opportunity the process gave an opposition to his government. However, international reports such as that issued by the International Crisis Group entitled "Reforming Egypt: In Search of a Strategy" said that presidential elections was a "false start." Also, the Brussels-based think tank criticized the opposition parties for being fragmented and urged them to unite on a common electoral platform.

The explosion of terrorism all over Egypt for a very long time made the government much preoccupied with security. It became one of the essential issues that cost much. But the regime did not try a political solution, not only towards terrorists themselves, but also towards moderate Islamist movements, and towards political parties in general.

It is obvious that complexities in North African countries are political, economic, and cultural. Hampered by very bad bilateral relations, States are trying to undermine internal and external risks. Despite clear differences, perfect democratic systems do not exist in any of the above-mentioned countries. This lack of democracy, transparency, and respect of human rights was the origin of extremism in its military, religious and ethnic facets, which endured economic underdevelopment with its high rates of illiteracy, unemployment, and poverty.

As a mean and a result, judicial systems are weak. So, human rights with their multi-dimensional aspects are not respected. It's clear that political theory has paved the way to improve the real facts of the power practice, but good governance is still a claim not only of political opposition and civil society, but also of international economic institutions, and to govern in "the right way" means to promote all the "institutional wreckage" in a country to be a State, a real State.

---

(1) The New York Times, International, August31st, 2000

(2) ROGER SCRUTON, Dictionary of Political Thought, second edition, 1996, MACMILLAN, p.365

(3) AIN MCLEAN, Oxford Concise Dictionary of Politics, 1996, Oxford University Press, p331

(4) See Cassier, The Myth of State, London, 1946.

(5) Niccolo Machiavelli, Te Prince (Le Prince), p67.

(6) Ibid. p.70.

(7) Ibid. p.76

(8) Ibid. p.86.

(9) Machiavelli gives the example of France, Ibid. pp 85-86.

(10) Ibid. p100.

(11) The end justifies the means.

(12) Christine Fame: "Les Declarations Des Droits de l'"Homme de 1789"
(1789's Human Rights declarations) ed; Petite Payot, pp61-92.

(13) Ibid. p.65.

(14) Ibid. p.70.

(15) Ibid. p.70.

(16) Ibid. p.77

(17) Ibid. p.82.

(18) Against dictatorship and personal rule or oligarchism, *shared power
systems* are political systems based on elected institutions and independence
of the judiciary, and an executive controlled by the legislative

(19) As it is in Spain and the United Kingdom.

(20) In many African countries some presidents declared themselves life
long presidents (e.g.) Habib Bourguiba in Tunisia (March 18th, 1975).

(21) Gregory H. Fox and Brad R. Roth, Democratic Governance and
International Law (Introduction: The Spread of Liberal Democracy),
2000, Cambridge University Press, p10.

(22) Universal Declaration of Human Rights, ART 21.

(23) Burdeau (George) "L'ETAT" (The State), p 17.

(24) International Covenant on Civil and Political Rights, Artic25.

(25) Ibid. Article 26.

(26) According to Article 40 of International Covenant on Civil and Political Rights, "The States Parties to the present Covenant undertake to submit reports on the measures they have adopted which give effect to the
rights recognized."

(27) UNDP, Re-conceptualizing Governance—Discussion paper 2, New
York, January 1977, pp 9-10.

(28) See http://www.civicus.org

(29) Ibid.

(30) Montesquieu "DE L'ESPRIT DES LOIS"—Book I, ed:.......p48.

(31) It's meant by North African countries in this research: Morocco,
Algeria, Tunisia, Libya, and Egypt.

(32) King Mohammed IV speech on July 30th, 1999.

(33) Since 1994, King Hassan II wanted to form a government of the
political parties who had never been in power, especially the USFP.

(34) Abdessalam Yassine, Enlightenment of women (Tanouir Almoumi-nat), Afak imp, Casablanca, 1997.

(35) Humbaraci (Arslan), Algeria: A Revolution that failed, A political History since 1954. New York: Praeger, 1966.

(36) http://www.jeuneafrique.com

Archives: Algeria

(37) When Chadli Benjdid resigned, the following presidents succeeded him: Khalid Nezar, Mohammed Boudiaf, Lyamin Zeroual, and Abdelaziz Bouteflika.

(38) Killings attended in March 2001 the number of 212 014 victims.

(39) Abassi Madani, a religious scholar, is more moderate than his colleague Ali Belhaj whose intentions to murder secular Algerians were publicly heard.

(40) Habib Souaidia. The Dirty War (La Salle Guerre), édition la decouverte, Paris, 2001.

(41) Arrests of human rights activists. More than this Tunisian authority censured "Le Monde", issue of April 6th, 2001 on which the Tunisian minister of human rights Salahedine Maaoui announced a complete change of the government policy of violation of human rights. See "Le Monde" 8/9 April, 2001.

(42) Tunisian official web site: http://www.tuinisia.gov

(43) Camille et Yves Lacoste, L'Etat du Maghrib, Ed. le Fennec, Casablanca, 1997, p74.

(44) FIDH and AMNESTY INTERNATIONAL annual reports of 2000.

(45) Kaddafi was openly supporting IRA during called war period.

(46) Hopwood (Derek) Egypt: Politics and Society, 1945–1984, Boston: Allen and Unwin, 1985.

(47) McDermott (Anthony). Egypt from Nasser to Mubarak: A flawed Revolution. London: Croom Helm, 1988.

(48) As a closed circle

(49) Deeb, Marius. Party politics in Egypt: the Wafd and Its Rivals, 1919–1939. London: State University of New York Press, 1971.

PART II

V. Political, Economic, and Judicial Systems

In past decades, the political and the economic spheres were the two major pillars of states' systems. But, in modern democracies, the judicial is determinant, if not the essential. It is the referee in society as a whole and especially for what is political and economic.

Whenever we find a free and fair judiciary, we can say that there are the seeds of democracy, accountability, and transparency. Also, the judicial system may be a medium of stability and development. Electoral disputes, civil servants misbehavior and corruption are brought in normal political conditions before the courts. If the justice is unfair or corrupt, judgments will be unjust. So, results of elections, however they are, they will be recognized as the official results and peoples' trust in government and the political elite may be destroyed. In this case stability will not be assured. Citizens may demonstrate violently and there may be large numbers of arrests. A parliament that is not drawn from fair elections cannot force accountability of the government and its agencies. An unfair election is made of many practices such as buying votes and falsifying the final results. A government established according to these kinds of elections cannot lead the country towards development. These kinds of governments struggle for their personal aims and ignore the public interest.

The re-conceptualizing of governance in North African countries means re-conceptualizing the political and economic system as a whole, but more than that it means re-conceptualizing the judicial system, and promoting civil society and human rights culture in a transparent and accountable atmosphere.

After the independence, North African countries were much preoccupied by consolidating institutions of the state and at the same time internal conflicts (1).

After assuring the macro standards of States, each North African country is trying to build its own experience by reforming and making renovations. Sometimes, these renovations were hurried, but other times they were more lagged than any one can imagine. Do they represent a real development, or just a veil to hide an ugly face?

Not only in North Africa, but from the Atlantic Ocean to the Red Sea, there are many religious political movements struggling for power. Most States are religious also, but with such modernism rejected by the Islamist activists (2).

---

(1) Camille et Yves Lacoste, L'Etat Du Maghrib (Encyclopedia), Ed. Le Fennec, Casablanca, 1991.

(2) Benjamin (Stora), Voies Singulieres pour Allier Islam et Modernite (Unique Ways to Rally Islam to Modernity), Ed. De l'Atelier, Paris, 1999.

-A-

MOROCCO:
HISTORICAL ROOTS, DEMOCRATIC WILL AND SCHIZOPHRENIC ELITES

1. Scrutinizing Elections

In 1997, after the parliamentary elections in Morocco, Mohammed Hafid an elected member of parliament resigned. He said that was because the administration falsified the final result in his favor. Mohammed Adib did the same. Opponent candidates to Adib and Hafid saying that their defeat was in an unfair elections brought the problem before the courts two days after the results were known, saying that their defeat was due to the interference in the electoral process. The constitutional court in charge of looking at these matters didn't pronounce on the two issues till two years after. It stated that Adib and Hafid were defeated and ordered to reorganize elections to fill these seats. This event let the public opinion suppose that many elected people know that they were falsely elected but they went on occupying the disputed seats.

Adib and Hafid were the first cases in Moroccan history where the elected members of parliament renounce to their declared success. The constitutional court was embarrassed, and for more than two years citizens of those circumscriptions were without representation in parliament. This is against article 2 of the constitution which stipulates that citizens should practice their sovereignty through institutions (1).

Unfortunately, Adib renounced to his decision and went to occupy his seat in the House of Representatives. At the same time, the constitutional court ordered the reorganization of election to occupy Hafid's seat. The candidate who was declared loser at the beginning was elected. Despite this incident, In Morocco the decade of the nineties has witnessed a great political change in Morocco.

The last King, Hassan II, initiated democratic development with constitutional reform in 1996, leading to the establishment of a directly elected Lower House of Parliament in 1997. As his party won the majority of seats in parliament, Abderrahman Alyoussoufi, Secretary General of the Socialist Union of the Popular Forces (USFP) and former opposition leader, became Prime Minister in 1998.

The National Democratic Institute (NDI) in its "political Overview" at that time about Morocco confirmed these developments, and added that "the accession of the young and reform-minded King Mohammed VI to the throne in July 1999 is a source of hope for increased political participation and democratic development" (2).

The left's engagement in the political process and peaceful struggle towards reform since 1972, and King Hassan's liberal convictions, contributed to democratic reforms reflected in the 1996 constitution (3). This is also due to the long and harsh struggle for democracy by the Moroccan people.

The bicameral legislature was created. The parliament consists of two Houses: the House of Representatives (Lower House) and the House of Councilors (Upper House or Senate) (4). Members of the Lower House are elected directly by universal suffrage for five-year term (5). The Upper House is elected by electoral colleges for nine years: three fifths by members elected in the regions of the country (local representatives), the other two-fifths are constituted by members elected by electoral colleges comprised of representatives of economic sectors and trade unions (6).

According to the earlier constitution, members of the House of Representatives (unicameral parliament) were to be elected for a six years term. It was composed of two thirds elected through direct universal suffrage, and the one third elected by an electoral college, also, comprised of representatives of economic sectors and trade unions (7).

The left suggested the abolition of the mentioned third. Hassan II accepted the idea of a parliament directly elected by universal suffrage, but created a whole House for that third: The House of Councilors. This house has the powers, either after long proceedings, to throw the government by censure motion (8).

In the 1996 Constitution, the Upper House was intended to secure equilibrium between political parties especially between the right wing and the left wing. When Hassan II named in 1998 the socialist Alyoussoufi Prime Minister, the Upper House was dominated by the rightists. After partial elections in September 2000, the majority represented in government dominated and centrists the National Rally of Independents (RNI) took the presidency of the House.

Also, by 1996 constitutional reforms, the High Audit Council was created. This made the whole financial policy of the state accountable. This council exercises the general supervision of the implementation of fiscal laws. It has to ensure the regularity of revenues and expenditure operations of departments legally falling under its jurisdiction, as it shall assess the management of the affairs thereof. It is empowered to penalize, if need be, any breach of the rules governing such operations (10).

According to the constitution, people exercise sovereignty directly, by means of referendum, or indirectly through constitutional institutions. Law is the supreme expression of the will of the Nation, and no limitation is to be put to the exercise of freedom of movement, opinion, and association except by law (11).

The King (The Commander of the Believers) is considered the guarantor of the perpetuation and the continuity of the State, who shall ensure the respect for the constitution, and be the protector of the rights and liberties of the citizens, social groups and organizations (12). The Moroccan crown is hereditary and handed down to descendants in direct male line and by order of primogeniture (13). The King appoints the Prime Minister who recommends to the King cabinet members to be appointed by him. The King may terminate their mandates or that of the government.

Parliament votes on legislation (14), and the right to introduce laws is granted equally by the Prime Minister and Members of Parliament (15). The government may declare the unsuitability of any proposal or amendment considered outside the purview of the legislative power. In case of disagreement either parliament or the government has to appeal the constitutional council. The King exercises, by royal decrees, the statutory powers explicitly conferred upon him by the constitution (16).

There is no clear idea in the constitution that makes the King obliged to appoint a Prime Minister from the majority, but the Lower House votes for his program. After the legislative elections of 2002, the King appointed as Prime Minister the minister of interior with no political party affiliation. Till 2005, no Prime Minister failed to win the majority, but all politicians assume that if he fails he has to resign and the king has to appoint another Prime Minister. Also, the Prime Minister suggests to the King names of ministers, but he hasn't the right to terminate their appointment, or to accept or refuse their resignation. These are prerogatives of the King. The people's political will expressed by vote is limited in influencing decision-making. The King is forced, but not obliged, to choose the prime minister from the majority. The parliament approves or disapproves the King's choice by vote. Another democratic step is needed to make the Prime Minister clearly drawn from the majority as it is done in established democracies.

The King appoints governors of administrative divisions. These governors are under the direct authority of the Interior Minister (18), and there is no constitutional possibility to influence the King's decision by vote. These governors have large prerogatives of control and policy making in the regions and the administrative divisions. They assume the coordination between all local departments and states' agencies. They are not accountable of their acts before any elected body. On the opposite, appointed governors supervise local elected councils. This is a limitation to democratic institutions.

Mayors are elected indirectly in big cities by municipal councilors who are directly elected by citizens. There is also the President of the Provinces who are elected by the same people in the same way, and the President of Regions that include many Provinces, who are elected also indirectly by district and, economic elected representatives, members of parliament within the region.

The local authority is under the governors' control, and the local electors' prerogatives are very limited. Representatives of ministries (health, finance, agriculture, industries etc…) run their policy directly with their central departments, which appoint them, and they do that under the supervision of governors, and they are members of the Provincial council that includes the mayor, the President of Provinces, and parliament members who belong to the same province. This local authority works with two staffs: the elected and the appointed. But the appointed dominates the elected in a regency way which is a huge handicap in the democratic practice (19).

2: Economy: Institutionalizing Modernity

In a special supplement to the "Foreign Policy" (summer 2000) sponsored by Moroccan and international firms, the Turkish professor of international relations at Koc University Bradford Dillman wrote: "Like the rest of the third world, Morocco suffers from high foreign debt, unemployment, and protection barriers. Reforms have been slow". The same publication adds: "high rates of unemployment and illiteracy will drag down growth. Poor public education, a lack of private schools, and a limited spread of English will hamper adaptation to the global information age".

This pre-paid article may be considered the most extremist political position in Morocco, especially when it wrote that "many in Morocco's political elite hope to transform the constitutional monarchy from one that rules to one that reigns".

But the analysis of the electoral process of 1997 may betray any extremist. The Turkish writer for the interest of the above-mentioned publication says that it was "free and fair", and extremists say that it was "neither free nor fair", though they recognize obvious developments.

King Hassan II said in one of his speeches that there are "those who eat in the house and insult its owner". Most of the active firms in Morocco—national and international ones—do not pay taxes. This situation has been going on since the independence in 1956. A corrupt and inactive public administration was the reason of this shame. When the traditional opposition came to power in 1998, it had declared a tax amnesty. The government said that this was to make a new beginning. All those who did not pay in the past, were not obliged to pay overdue taxes. But since that year everyone has started to pay.

Corruption exists on a wide range. The national section of Transparency International described the situation as disastrous. Both private and public sectors are blamed of this plague. Government leads from time to time anti-corruption drives. Many officials were arrested, but all of them were from middle and low ranks. Never a minister was blamed for corruption.

Economy is an area of heated controversy between political parties. From the economic point of view, all political parties are liberals. Some activists make the difference between corrupted and uncorrupted political parties. The two main economic views are between socialists themselves represented by Fatahlah Oualalou and Habib Malki. Both are famous scholars. The first considers that inflation rates and budget deficit should be kept stabilized as lower as possible. This means assuring stability of national currency (Dirhame), intervention of equalization fund to assure equilibrium between supply and demand to help maintaining the economic stability, which is the forward step toward development. The second considers that dropping the market, and investing savings, and devaluation of national currency is to encourage investments especially international ones and since then we can get low unemployment rates, and high development rates. King Hassan II used to believe in the first thesis. When he called the opposition to form the government, he named Oualalou Minister of Economy and Finance, and his rival was named minister of agriculture.

While discussing his first budget within government in 1998, Malki gave utterance to his thoughts. Some ministers supported him, but after long discussions that were reflected in the press, it was decided to take up Oualalou's view. Asian breakdown and international financial turmoil helped to convince other ministers about the need for internal and external stability. This internal and external stability was welcomed by the Executive Board of IMF in its conclusions after consultation with Morocco, and more than that, IMF stated that "the draft budget for financial year 1999/2000 could have set a more ambitious target for deficit reduction."

One of the main aims of the government was to reduce Morocco's external debt burden. After prudent external borrowing and active debt management policy, the government succeeded in reducing Morocco's external debt, including through refinancing and early repayment of expensive loans and debt-equity swaps.

Since1980, Moroccan economy underwent deep change. Adjustment Program welcomed (or ordered) by IMF deepened the liberal tendencies of the market, and prepared the country to a new privatization law (1989) that was the origin of a long-term privatization program that started in 1993.

Privatization law provides that transfers and operations are to be completed through financial market procedures. The government sets price, judicial and financial forms. Employees are invited to participate. Since the operation launched in 1993, 58 entities have been transferred, including 35 companies and 23 hotels. In 2000 revenues from privatization were 1.7billion dollars. Foreign investors have participated, especially in strategic sectors such as energy and petroleum. Their employees have purchased twelve of the privatized companies.

Public finance was also reformed in the 1980s. Taxes on businesses, revenue taxes and value-added-taxes are along with other general taxes the principal components of the fiscal system. Company tax rates are fixed at 35 per cent (36.9 per cent for stable credit establishment, 12 per cent for foreign establishment in real estate, technical and industrial establishment, 10 per cent for solid foreign establishment in materials).

Those who seek to create a business are exempt from taxes during the first three years. After a three-year period, taxes are applicable at a 6 per cent rate for liberal professions, 0.5 per cent for all other activities and 0.25 per cent for activities selling petrol products, gas, butter, oils, sugar and flour. Agricultural activities are exonerated from taxes till 2010.

Since 1992, Morocco has tried to make the payment of its debt a priority. The external debt fell from 128.4 per cent to 36.6 per cent in 1998. The government has concluded agreements with the French and Spanish governments by which they dropped parts of their debts. According to this agreement the government had to invest an equal amount of money in social projects.

Tourism and Moroccans living abroad brought together in 1999, 34.8 billion Dirhams to the national budget. Phosphates, fish sales brought 19.3 billion Dirhams. In 2006, Morocco has been making of tourism one of the highest priorities. It had launched the strategy to receive 10 Millions by 2010.

The structural adjustment plan (SAP) led to a new banking law (promulgated on July 6th, 1993 replacing a former law dating back to 1967. This new law built the legal framework applicable to all credit establishments and opened to them new domains such as credit-lease, building and construction, managing assistance, etc.

Bank AL-Maghrib is the central bank. It is a public establishment with a civil profile and financial autonomy. It manages the nation's exchange reserves and can operate as a commercial bank.

In Morocco there are 21 banks and 56 finance companies. The banking system is rapidly modernizing with the rest of the world's modern banking institutions. It has introduced new means of payment such as on-line payment cards and ATM's. Some banks have even begun offering interest-banking services to their clients.

With regard to the convertibility of the national currency (Dirhame) operators have free buying access to currencies quoted by Bank AL-Maghrib for settling of all common transactions, without need for Exchange Office permission.

Foreign investors benefit from convertibility plan guaranteeing freedom to realize investment projects without a pre-existent exchange plan and they are free to transfer investment revenue (after required taxes) without limit.

IMF welcomed Moroccan monetary policy. It said, "Financial system was sufficiently sound so as not to pose serious financial risks for the economy." But at the same time, it encouraged (strongly) the authorities to continue monitoring closely developments in the financial sector.

Social conditions are severely criticized by trade unions. Lowest wages are about 150 dollars per month. This is what law provides. In reality, there are less than 50 dollars per month. NGOs criticize the bad living conditions of most of the social classes. They say that the government did nothing to alleviate unemployment and illiteracy (47 per cent). It was estimated that 100.000 households lived below the poverty line and the profile of poverty was vividly seen in rural areas. The UNDP indicator on poverty had placed Morocco in the 125th place. Two official foundations (Mohamed V Foundation and Hassan II Foundation) make some efforts by helping poor people to earn their living, but they are very far to respond to the huge need in the country.

Though the elections of 2002 were the most fair in Moroccan history, they had no effect on the economic situation in the country. Most of the main economic projects were led by the King Mohammed VI himself.

3: The Judicial System: Longing for Independence

The organization of the Moroccan judicial system is a function of the Moroccan constitution. By virtue of Article 82 of the constitution, the judiciary is independent from the legislative and the executive powers. Sentences are passed and executed in the King's name. The King appoints magistrates by Royal Decrees upon recommendations made by the Supreme Council of Magistracy, which is headed by the King. This council consists of: a) the Minister of justice as vice-president, b) the chief justice of the Supreme Court, c) the attorney general in the Supreme Court, d) the president of the first chamber of Supreme Court, e) two representatives elected among the magistrates of the Court of Appeal, f) four representatives elected among the magistrates of first degree courts. The Council of Magistracy ensures the promotion and punishment of judges.

The Constitutional council consists of: a) six members appointed by the King for a period of nine years; b) six members for the same period, three appointed by the President of the House of Representatives, and three others appointed by the President of the House of Councilors, upon consultation with the parliamentary groups.

One-third of each category of the members of the Constitutional Council is renewed every three years. The King chooses the Chairperson of the Constitutional Council among the members he appoints. The term of office of the Chair and members of the Constitutional Council are not renewable. The constitution Council determines the constitutionality of laws. Before promulgation, the King, the Prime Minister, the President of the House of Councilors, or one-fourth of the Members of either House, may for the same reason, refer laws to the Constitutional Council.

The High Court of Justice may try members of Government who may be indicted by either the House of Parliament and referred to it for trial. Government members have penal responsibilities for crimes and felonies that they might commit while exercising their functions.

Every person has the right to be protected by justice and to sue others and be sued. There are two levels of jurisdiction that enable people to ask for appeal, and hearings are public.

The second tribunal, the tribunal of appeal includes, under the authority of the first president many chambers specialized including those in charge of personnel status and inheritance cases, and those in charge of criminals. Three judges make the decisions. The court of appeal has the ability to uphold or refuse decisions of the first instance.

Courts of trade were created in 1995. There is the first court and the court of appeal. They look at all what concerns trade, either between its agents or what is related to their action. Like all judicial systems, there are important auxiliary parties.

The auxiliary parties in the Moroccan justice system are the clerks, registrars, experts, translators and attorneys. The clerks and registrars are responsible for the day-to-day functioning office order and the secretary's office of the public ministry. They are also responsible for the co-ordination of services within its control.

The attorneys are present to introduce the parties in dispute before the justice system in order to assure the defense of clients. For that, they can bring all action, open procedures and intervene and secure the follow-up of the execution of judgments rendered by the tribunal and give advice and legal consulting.

As Arabic is the official language in Morocco, when in court indigenous people speak only Tamazight, they should look for a translator. Unfortunately, there were no sworn translators of Tamazight, while there were many for international languages. Some say that Tamazight speaking people shouldn't be treated as foreigners, but really some Moroccan citizens (Imazighen) can't understand the language in which they are tried, and they cannot afford a translator. Fair justice needs the opposite. The king Mohammed VI ordered on 30 July 2001 to assure sworn translators in Tamazight to Imazighen.

Human right's NGOs used to consider this a sort of discrimination especially against local illiterate population. This was not the first and last problem in Moroccan justice, there are also problems related to independence and corruption.

Ex-minister Aziman talked about corruption. More than this, it is reported by some of his counselors that Hassan II appointed him minister of justice, after the King requested him as a scholar to carry out a research project on the administration of justice and Aziman reached the conclusion that justice is corrupted and dependent. Instead of being evicted, the King named him minister of justice. This was considered a high recognition of the justice-deteriorated situation and the need for its reform.

So, we imagine that he is there to make it fair, strong, and independent. But when the minister declared in a conference in Casablanca that "justice is corrupted", a storm of opposition blew all over rightist lobbies, and they succeeded to bring the minister himself before the parliament to apologize.

Attorneys' association called in a national meeting in fez (November 23rd,–24th, 2000) for an urgent reform to justice and said that this "depends on the political will" and "moralizing and reforming mechanisms of the state."

---

(1) Kingdom of Morocco, The Constitution of 1996, published by the Ministry of Communication October 1996, ART. P6.

(2) National Democratic Institute, Morocco "Political Overview. http://www.ndi.org (see worldwide activities).

(3) Memorandum of the Koutla (coalition of traditional opposition parties) presented to the King Hassan II in 1996.

(4) The Constitution, ART.4.

(5) Ibid. ART. 37

(6) Ibid. ART. 38

(7) Ibid. ART. 43

(8) Ibid. ART. 77

(9) Ibid. ART. 98

(10) Ibid. ART. 96

(11) Ibid. ART. 11

(12) Ibid. ART. 19

(13) Ibid. ART. 20

(14) Ibid. ART. 54

(15) Ibid. ART. 52

(16) Ibid. ART

(17) Ibid.

(18) In 1998 Hassan II appointed the socialist Alyoussoufi Prime Minister, and appointed the Ministers of Interior, justice, foreign Affairs, and Islamic Affairs. Mohammed VI kept the same authority over these ministries, although he damaged some ministers.

(19) Mohamed IV declared in an official speech that this kind of regency is a handicap to democracy and to development.

-B-

ALGERIA:
OIL AND POVERTY WITHOUT DEMOCRACY

1. Failure of Democracy

During the 1990s, Algeria lived the hardest experience in its history. Civil war declared by the Islamic movement put the whole country in an oven. The political system in all its levels vanished, and paved the way to violence, and terrorist activities. At the beginning of the third millennium, observers started to ask another question: who is behind massive Killings in Algeria? Are they really Islamic groups, the Algerian official police, or the Popular National Army (1)?

In January 1992, the military obliged President Chadli Benjdid to resign, and stopped an electoral process that was going on to give majority to the Islamist party the Islamic Salvation Front (FIS) (2).

As a socialist regime, Algerian officials were against any government to be formed by an Islamic movement. The 1988's constitution, amended in 1992, brought pluralism without preparing the institutional groundwork for democracy (3). Early Steps towards liberalism led by President Chadli Benjdid had never meant democracy and freedom of expression (4).

Military Generals had the habit to choose the president of the state. As members of the ex-unique party National Liberation Front (FLN), they were influencing the choice of candidates to the Popular Assembly (Parliament). When the Islamists got the majority after the first round of a two rounds electoral system, Generals were unready to let them go to the second round and win legislative elections. If they did, they would have the possibility to form government.

During the unique party rule, Islamists were either in jail or denied the right to express themselves. After the establishment of pluralism, they started harsh campaigns against the state's high officials including generals.

Afraid of being arrested and executed by a supposed future Islamic government supported by Chadli Benjdid, Generals forced the president to resign, and the FIS was banned. After that, they went on to prepare the new constitution in which it is stated clearly that political parties shouldn't be based on Islam or on any ethnic group.

Under this provision, it wasn't possible for the FIS to come back to the political scene. The Gathering for Culture and Democracy (RCD), and the Socialist Forces Front (FFS), though they are based essentially on the Kabili ethnic groups, they were not outlawed, but they faced many difficulties.

Hamas (the Peace Society Movement) was named Islamic Society Movement. It has changed its name according to the organic law governing political parties, as amended on March 6th, 1997. Article 3 of this law states that political parties, in their activities, must refrain using Islam and Berber for the political party's goals.

Algeria wasn't prepared for a democracy. The constitution was revised in November 1988 after violent demonstrations in streets, which pushed 17 prominent personalities to sign a declaration asking for democracy (5).

Pluralism was introduced in the 1988 constitution after 26 years of unique party system. Three years after, citizens were called to vote. Democracy wasn't properly rooted. Long years of oppression put public feelings at the top. Hoping to eradicate the unique party, they were nearly ready to eradicate the new pluralistic system as a whole.

Islamists were not clear in their views about democracy. They were considering it a foreign idea. They were calling for "Ashoura" (6), but this position did not forbid them to go to elections, and the Algerians voted for them in December 1991 at the first round election.

Frightened by the Islamist arrival to power, military Generals led by Gen. Khalid Nezar obliged Chadli Benjdid to resign and formed the "High committee of State" (HCS). The state of emergency was declared. A rotating presidency between HCS members led Khalid Nezar to be the tougher man of the country. In 1994, HCS brought from Morocco an old Algerian resistance fighter called Mohamed Boudiaf who had participated in the liberation war against France, and proposed to him to be president of Algeria. Before this year, and for more than 30 years, the man had chosen to live in a small town called Kenitra (north of the Moroccan capital Rabat).

The historical conflict between Algeria and Morocco made commentators in the region astonished to the military generals' choice. The man accepted to be president. He left Morocco, and had left his wife and children behind. Shortly afterwards he was shot dead by an army officer. Boudiaf, the President, was killed in his presidential chair while addressing a speech about the need of a national struggle against corruption. The shooter was arrested, but years after his death, those who urged the officer to kill the president were never known.

It was thought that Boudiaf was the savior, but after his death in 1994, the shadow of decay came back. After hesitations HCS chose another military high official, Gen. Lyamin Zeroual, to be president.

Between 1992 and 1994, violence ravaged the country. Thousands of casualties were registered. Whole families were harshly slaughtered. Either in cities or in countryside, people were living in terror.

Lyamin Zeroual was decided to exterminate violent Islamist movements. Islamic Salvation Front's (FIS) army branch (AIS) declared its responsibility for many violent activities. Islamic-Armed Groups (GIA)—extremist wing of AIS—was more violent in its attacks. Many other armed groups were born. The scene got more and more harsh and violent. In April 1994, the government decided that citizens should take arms to defend themselves. 200.000 rifles were distributed under strict control of military, local authorities and ex-unique party members (7).

When Zeroual declared that the presidential elections were to be organized in November 1995, no one was sure that he would succeed in keeping Algeria in peace that day. But he did. He not only succeeded in making elections safe from any threat, but he succeeded to be the first elected Algerian president in a pluralistic election by 61 per cent followed by Mahfoud Nahnah (25 per cent) who was the candidate of all moderate Islamists groups (8).

Instead of calming the situation, the success of the presidential elections pushed extremist armed groups to show their strength. Small towns were exterminated, high officials were killed in front of their children, and seven monks were savagely killed; two months after they were kidnapped from their monastery in Algiers.

Some politicians say that the elections were in themselves just a way to turn the Algerian public opinion away from the National Charter Group that drafted vainly a peace plan in Rome (Saint 'Egidio). One of its proposals to resolve the situation was to bring peacefully back the FIS to the national scene. This was sufficient for Army Generals to reject the whole plan, and all the pro-military elite had to follow (9).

Although he was elected, and the army signed an agreement with AIS in October 1997, Lyamin Zeroual wasn't able to crack down armed groups. So, he decided to resign, and called for new presidential elections.

Many candidates were in the new race. Abdelaziz Bouteflika, Ahmed Taleb Ibrahimi, Abdullah Saâd Jeballah, Hussein Aït Ahmed, Mouloud Hamrouch, Mokdad Sifi, and Youssef Alkhatib led harsh campaign, but at the election eve they withdraw and left Bouteflika alone and blamed him of being the candidate of the Algerian Army Security (AAS).

Bouteflika had been in dispute with some generals at the end of the 1970s. Gen. Khalid Nezar evicted him in 1979 from the National Liberation Front (FLN). At that time, it was the ruling party. Before the presidential elections in November 1999, the General met Ahmed Taleb Ibrahimi, the first rival to Bouteflika, and asked him about his conditions to succeed Zeroual. According to the information gathered by "*Le Nouvel Afrique Asie*", Ibrahimi said that he would be a candidate if the army was to let him manage freely internal and external affairs, and let the army just assure security and independence of the state (10). Nezar's failure to convince Ibrahimi to cooperate with the army, freed Gen. Laarbi Belkhir to call retired high officers to vote for Bouteflika (11).

Algeria's decay encouraged all national political partners, Generals first, to look for a personality who was able to make Algerians recall the past years of stability and the strength of the state. Bouteflika was seen as the shadow of Houary Boumedien (12). As democracy was not on any one's agenda, Hussein Aït Ahmed the historical leader of the opposition, who has been calling for democracy since the socialist age and during one-party rule, was looked at as a politician who came before his time. Mahfoud Nahnah was more convincing. Compared to other Islamist extremists, he was seen a moderate who might be an alternative to Abassi Madani and Ali Belhaj, the two famous leaders of Islamic Salvation Front (FIS). Generals did not gave Nahnah their support, may be because they felt that he was not able to handle the situation firmly as may be done by the shadow of Boumedien. When the dice was cast, the military forces were behind Bouteflika. He was considered candidate of military security agency.

On 12 February 1999, when Zeroual announced the presidential calendar elections, he tried to make generals set aside. "No one has the right to speak in the name of the State's institutions unless he is legally able to do that", he averted. Nezar who felt pointed at retorted some minutes later saying that "riddance is not at the appropriate moment". Nezar and retired generals supported Bouteflika. They considered him "the less bad" (13).

Bouteflika would have never hoped to be president if civil war did not take place. By supporting Bouteflika, the military wanted a civilian as President, and the army to come back to the second position. Soldiers, policemen, public sector employees, "nationals" are about 2 millions (20per cent of voters) (14). This is the mass to be mobilized whenever needed by state lobbies.

On April 15th, Bouteflika was alone in the head of the race. The final results were the following:

a. Abdelaziz Bouteflika—independent ex-minister of foreign affairs: 73.3 per cent;

b. Ahmed Taleb Ibrahimi—ex-minister of foreign affairs supported by Islamists: 12.54 per cent;

c. Abdullah Jeballah—Annahda dissident presented independent: 3.96 per cent;

d. Mouloud Hamrouch—ex-Prime Minister during Chadli Benjdid's presidency: 3.11 per cent;

e. Mokdad Sifi—ex-prime minister of Zeroual: 2.24 per cent;

f.   Youssef Khatib—a leader of liberation army:1.20 per cent;

g.   Hussein Aït Ahmed—President of FFS: 0.32 per cent;

In 1995, the presidential elections that were held on November 16th, gave Lyamin Zeroual 61.01 per cent of the vote and thus defeated Mahfoud Nahnah, his closest competitor with 25.67 per cent of vote.

After Lyamin Zeroual election in 1995, many political parties participated in government including moderate Islamists of Nahnah who had seven ministers (15). So, breaking with total technocratic governments was on the way since 1995. When Ahmed Benbitour resigned, Bouteflika kept the coalition of four parties in government (FLN, RND, Annahda, and MSP).

Bouteflika kept the government of his predecessor for six months, before calling Ahmed Benbitour to form his government. Shortly after, Benbitour resigned because the "president didn't respect his PM prerogatives."

Benflis, Bouteflika brother-in-law, was appointed prime minister. Although he was one of the founders of the Algerian League of Human Rights in 1987 (16), the new PM kept good relations with Generals. His man was the retired General Laarbi Belkhir. When appointed director of Bouteflika presidential campaign, Belkhir guaranteed the support of the army. After Benflis left the president's staff, Belkhir occupied it, which is a remarkable sign of the weight that army has in the Algerian modern politics.

Bouteflika led a harsh struggle against Benflis who was one of the six candidates that met the requirements dictated by the electoral law. The FLN was divided between the two rival candidates. Abdelazizi Belkhadem led a wing that supported Bouteflika, while Benflis who was newly elected secretary general found himself with the minority. In the presidential elections that took place in April 2004, Bouteflika received 83.5 per cent of the vote. Benflis resigned and Belkhadem was named secretary general of the FLN. As a reward, Bouteflika named his supporter vice-president.

The political system in Algeria provides that soldiers, all ranks included, vote in elections, which is different from Morocco where they vote in referendums about constitutions only. Bouteflika was supposed to be the first civilian president "much loved" by the military apparatus. He was the first president who used his fluency in Arabic to depict the military role in Algerian modern history in vivid poetic words that any soldier has never heard.

"La concorde civil" (Amnesty law) was Bouteflika's main project. It is based on surrender of armed groups in exchange of amnesty. Before his arrival to presidency, the background was prepared to that. In October 1997, the army concluded an agreement with the Salvation Islamic Army (AIS), by which the last party suspended its army struggle.

What was difficult, before 1997, was for a statesman to think about a possible arrangement with "killers". Once Started, it had to go till the end, so it was thought.

What was new for Bouteflika was to make an agreement between two rival groups: the army and the Islamists. This was a popular step that was hoped for to end violence. For this he started a countrywide campaign for a referendum, which asked the Algerian people if he would grant amnesty to armed groups.

Although diverse armed groups were involved in the bloody conflict, the majority of Algerians voted amnesty law (17). It was a success to a new president who declared himself devoted to reforming the political system.

In July 2005, Bouteflika called to a new referendum for a new amnesty law. This was criticized by local NGOs who were blaming security forces for being behind the disappearances between 1993 and 2003. Though the government established an ad hoc mechanism on the disappeared, victims' families criticized bitterly what they called "the government will to hide the truth." Safia Fahassi, a spokeswoman for the Algerian Coordination of the Families of the Disappeared said that: "They think they can tear the pages of 10 years of violence from our memory, give us money and make us forget about our disappeared." Fahassi said her husband, a journalist, was kidnapped in May 1995 and was never found.

The Algerian political system is based on the 1976 constitution amended in 1989 when the multi-party system was set. The actual constitution was voted on November 28th, 1996 in which more amendments were included. The legislature detailed pluralism conditions in a very long article [42]. After stating that "the right to create political parties is acknowledged and guaranteed", it adds that "this right cannot be put forward to infringe upon fundamental liberties, values and fundamental components of national identity, to security, territorial unity, independence of state, people's sovereignty, to democratic and republican aspects of state." The same article adds that "political parties shouldn't to be founded on religious, linguistic racial, and sexual, corporatist or regional basis."

The president should be not only an Algerian by birth, but his wife should be from the same nationality also. If he was born before July 1942, he has to prove that he participated to November 1st, 1954 revolution. And if he was born after July 1942, he has to prove that his parents did not participate in any hostile act to the same revolution.

One of the prerogatives of the president is to appoint high officials, judges, and governors of regions. The president appoints ministers, but the prime minister selects them first (article 79). After being appointed, the prime minister has to submit to the National Popular Assembly (APN) his program. If it isn't approved, he has to resign (Art. 80 and 81). At that moment, the president has to name another prime minister, and APN has to vote for the new prime minister's program or to be dissolved. President can dissolve APN after a referendum (Art.87).

Though the Constitution ensures the government's prerogatives, they were never fully practiced. On the opposite, Algeria is experiencing a liberal gradual change, but the constitution provides the socialist regime. For this reason, the IMF urged Algeria to amend the constitution by changing article 17 to make the free market a constitutional provision.

2. Economic System: Chaos of the Public Sector

When he was answering to a journalist's question, Ahmed Tibaoui minister in charge of Participation (privatization) said that "privatizing is like selling a used car". So, he thought that he had to "bring it up to be in a working order."

Algerian socialism was called the "capitalism of state," which was in reality a sort of "capitalism of high personalities of state." Generals influenced not only politics but economy also. They were opposed to army openness towards liberalism (18). Clung to traditional third world socialism, liberal ideas were banned. Mahfoud Nahnah and many scholars were arrested in the 1970s just because they were preaching for the private sector and the right of private ownership. When the Soviet System collapsed, Algeria found itself in the dark. IMF lit a candle of hope and politicians followed. They had no other choice (19).

The Algerian economy remains heavily dependent on the petroleum sector, which accounts for about one quarter of GDP, and contributes slightly more than half of government revenues, and virtually all of the export receipts. As a result, oil prices have great impact, either positive or negative, on the overall macroeconomic situation (20).

After the implementation of IMF supported programs, between 1994 and 1998, Algeria was successful in restoring macroeconomic stability and implementing structural reforms. In its consultation report (21), IMF concludes, "in 1999, activity in the non-hydrocarbon sectors slowed down wile inflation performance improved. Real growth decreased to 3.3 per cent in 1999 from 5.1 per cent in 1998 despite a strong performance in the hydrocarbon sector (6.2 per cent). Non-hydrocarbon GDP increased by only about 2.5 per cent growth in 1998. In particular—IMF adds—activity in the agricultural sector and in the industrial public sector decelerated, which was mainly due to adverse weather conditions and continued structural deficiencies. Against this background and owing to a labor force growth of about 3 per cent per annum, the unemployment rate has probably continued to increase to about 30 per cent. The consumer price index (CPI) rose by only 2.6 per cent on average in 1999 following a 5.0 percent increase in 1998. A part of the 1999 deflation is attributed to lower food prices."

Reforms initiated in 1999 concern also the banking system to new domestic and foreign banks. Similarly, minority stakes in the three public sector companies were listed in 1999 on the newly—created Algiers Stock Exchange. However, changes in tariff positions and the introduction since

1997 of minimum dutiable values for selected imports have resulted in increased effective protection.

Under the mercy of oil prices that rose in the year 2000, the president of the republic added between 10 and 15 per cent in wages. But the fall of 1998 and the first half of 1999 demanded the cutting budget expenditure, the exchange rate was allowed to depreciate vis-à-vis the US dollar; and real interest rates were kept high. Despite this harsh situation, these policies were important in limiting the depletion of foreign exchange reserves and consolidating the fiscal position.

New liberals consider that maintenance of a high degree of growth would help Algeria very much. They expressed frankly their views about accelerating trade liberalization both on a regional and multilateral basis. Mouloud Hamrouch was the first prime minister to declare openly that the liberation of national economy was an inevitable choice. When he was forced to resign in 1989, he said that he paid the price for his courage to "start to practice a new economic theory based on free market, or what we call today a recommended liberalism" (22).

In the socialist systems, private property was seen as a threat to stability or more than that a threat to the nation, if not a treason. The same was for the Algerian case. Therefore managerial staffs of different firms were hoping for a free market system to improve their living, or to become owners of their private firms.

3. Judicial System: The Weight of the Uniform

According to the constitution, the judicial system is "independent and practiced according to laws." Sentences are passed in public, executed in the name of the people, and the administration can be sued (ART.143). The miscarriages of justice entail reparation by the state. Judges are protected against all forms of intervention. They are accountable by the high council of judges. The high court regulates the activities of the administrative jurisdiction. Both assure unification of jurisdiction. The law punishes authority abuse (ART.22).

The President of state is also president of the high council of judges that proposes to him to whom to offer amnesty as a presidential right. A high court of state is to be instituted to acknowledge acts that may be considered as a high treason of the president for crimes and offences committed by the prime minister in the discharge of his duties (23).

Though pluralism was included, the 1996 constitution declares in its preamble that the National Liberation Front, the ex-unique party, "played by its sacrifices an important role in the independence of the country." Actually, the same party is only one of a large number of parties that form the actual political scene in modern Algeria. This shows that in many countries politics has nothing to do with laws (24).

---

(1) Habib Souadia, The Dirty War (La Salle Guerre), édition le decouverte, Paris, 2001.

(2) "Islam, Democracy, and the State: The Reemergence of Authoritarian Politics in Algeria," paper presented at 18th Annual Symposium, Center for Contemporary Arab Studies, Georgetown University on "Islam and Secularism in North Africa," Washington, April 1–2, 1993.

(3) I. William Zartman, "Algeria: Technocratic Rule, Military Power" in Political elite in Arab North Africa: Morocco, Algeria, Tunisia, Libya, and Egypt, New York: Longman, 1982, pp: 92-143.

(4) "Algeria under Chadli: Liberalization without Democratization or Perestroika, Yes; Glasnost, No," in Middle East Insight, 6, No.3, 1988, pp: 47-64.

(5) http://www.jeuneafrique.com

(6) *"Ashoura"* comes from the prophet Mohammed saying that "matters of people are subjects of discussions between them". It is the first principle of governance that was implemented by the prophet Mohammed. It used to mean that there shouldn't be an authoritative rule, and every one has the right to participate in decision-making. But this was a customary law as it is not institutionalized. Some Islamic movements say in these days that Democracy is against Islam as it has *"Ashoura"*, but they forget that the

essence of "*Ashoura*" is the participation of the community in making decisions; which is one of the basic rules in Democracy.

(7) http://www.lemonde.fr

(8) www.ICL, Algeria Index.

(9) http://www.liberation.com

(10) Ibid.

(11) Jeune Afrique l'Inteligent No.2014/2015, 17–30 August 1999, p.43.

(12) Houary Boumedien, President of Algeria from 1964 till 1978.

(13) General Nezar fled arrest in Paris in May 2001 for "crimes against humanity."

(14) The soldiers represent 20 per cent of votes.

(15) Society Movement of peace: http://www.hms-algeria.net

(16) Jeune Afrique l'Inteligent, No. 2014, 17–20 August 1999, p42.

(17) GIA, the Army, Police, Groups of Legitimate defense (200.000 who were offered arms for self defense), AIS. See Jeune Afrique l'Inteligent, No.2014/2015, 17–30 August 1999.

(18) http://www.algeria-watch.org/en/hr/victims_groups.htm

(19) Ottawa, David B., and Marina Ottaway, "Algeria: The Politics of socialist revolution," Berkley: University of California Press, 1970. See also Boukhobza, Mohamed, "Reptures et Transformations Sociales en Algerie" (The Cut and Social Transformation in Algeria) Algiers: office des publications universities, 1989.

(20) IMF

(21) IMF, Press release no.99/19, May 26th, 1999.

(22) IMF conclusions (Article IV consultation with Algeria 7 public information Notice (PIN) no.00/54, August 4th, 2000.

(23) See note number 15.

(24) Jeune Afrique l'Inteligent, No.2014/2015, 17–30 August 1999, p33.

(25) Algerian Constitution of November 28th, 1996, Chapter III: Judiciary, Articles from 138 till 158.

-C-

TUNISIA:
PLURALISM OF THE UNIQUE
AND THE POSTPONED DEMOCRACY

1. No Right to True Candidacy to Presidency

In 1997, seven years after his coup d'Etat against Habib Bourguiba ex-life long president of Tunisia (since 1955), Zinalabidin Benali declared that he wanted pluralistic presidential elections in 1999 (1).Before that a new electoral law was published. It stated that there is only "ONE" condition for Tunisian citizens to be candidates. This "ONE" condition is explained through three requirements are:

a.   To be head of a political party;

b.   To occupy this position at least for five years on the day of submission of candidacy;

c.   To be supported by at least thirty deputies or presidents of local elected councils (2).

It is obvious that the right to be candidate to presidency is not everyone's right. And these triple conditions excluded the two prominent opposition movements: The movement of Democratic Socialism (MDS) and the Islamic Movement Tendency (Annahda). Ismail Boulahia the secretary general of MDS occupied this position for less than three years, and Annahda was completely outlawed since 1988 (3). Benali was re-elected president on October 24th, 1999 without any difficulty. His two rivals were only shadows of president Benali himself, as they were supporting his policy. These two candidates are Mohammed Belhaj Amor of the Popular Union Party (PUP) and Abderrahman Tlili of Democratic Union Party (UDU). The opposition wasn't represented.

The Tunisian officials are very proud of this experience. They present it as the first pluralistic presidential election in Tunisian history, which is in some sense true. Despite that, it wasn't totally so. Bourguiba was the unique candidate in 1959, 1964, 1969 and 1974. When he expired the four constitutional terms (constitution of July 1st, 1959), under his orders, the National Assembly (Parliament) named him on March 18th, 1975 life long president. Tunisians didn't go back to ballots till Bourguiba was forced to resign. For this reason Benali thinks that Tunisians should be happy to be granted a minimal kind of democracy; a position that human rights activists consider senseless as democracy isn't a gift by the rulers but a right of the people (4).

In 1994, Benali was the only candidate to the presidential elections. No Tunisian could get the support of 30 big electors a *sine qua non* condition at that time to be candidate. In 1999, he was re-elected for five years in a "semi-pluralist" ballot. More than institutional democracy, the political one is far of being reached. The real opposition activists are either in prison or in exile. No critique is tolerated against the president of state. The press isn't independent and it is tolerated to insult the opposition leaders without giving them the right to reply (5).

On October 24th, 2004, the presidential and legislative elections confirmed Benali's hegemony. His party, the RCD got 152 seats and 37 (out of 189) were divided between 5 opposition parties. The local NGOs criticized the lack of media access by opposition candidates. According to the amendments to the electoral law, 20 percent of seats were reserved to members of the opposition political parties.

Many exiled personalities including the ex-prime minister Mohammed Mzali declared that they didn't want to come back to their country because they are afraid of being brought before the courts without being accorded the right to self-defense. They give the example of Khemais Chamari who himself lives in exile. He is the lawyer who defended Mohamed Mouaâda an ex-secretary general of MDS before the court and who was blamed by the authorities of disclosing details of the instruction. The same opponents say that they are afraid of being violently treated, and prevented from moving freely (6). Despite this situation, the constitution provides for liberties of opinion, expression, the press, publication, assembly, and association (7). The political system guarantees basic freedom, but limits them by specific rules that suppress in practice these rights as it is for the electoral law.

The bicameral system was instituted in 2005. The upper house was elected in June 2005. The National Parliament (NP) exercises the legislative power. Its members are elected by "universal, free, direct and secret suffrage." People who are at least twenty-five years of age on the day of submission of candidacy are eligible to serve in parliament. The NP is elected for a period of five years. In circumstances of war or any peril, a presidential law may extend its mandate until the time it would be possible to proceed with elections (8).

Immunity is assured and deputies can't be prosecuted, arrested, or tried for opinions expressed, proposals made, or acts carried out in the exercise of their mandate in the NP. To arrest a deputy or to prosecute him during his mandate for crime or misdemeanor, parliament has to lift the immunity that covers him. However, in the event of being caught in the act, arrest procedure is permitted. In such a case, the NP is to be informed "without delay". The detention of a deputy is suspended if the NP requests so (9).

Parliament exercises the legislative power, and NP may authorize the president of the republic to issue decree-laws within a "fixed time limit and for a specific purpose which must be submitted for ratification to the NP upon expiration of that time limit." The NP votes organic laws (at the latest by December 31) (10).

In accordance with the first article of the constitution by which Tunisia's religion is Islam, the president should be a Muslim and Tunisian. His father, mother and paternal and maternal grandfather (all of them) should be of Tunisian nationality without interruption (11).

The president is elected for five years by the universal suffrage within the last thirty days of the serving president. The president himself is a member of the commission witch enrolls candidates. The other members are the president of NP and some presidents of the judicial corps. The president is the chairman of this commission that validates candidates, and proclaims the results of the ballot (12).

The president of the republic nominates the Prime Minister, and on his proposal, the other members of government. He presides over the council of ministers, and dismisses the government or one of its members on his own initiative or on the recommendation of the Prime Minister. He promulgates laws, watches over their execution and he may return the bill to the NP for a second reconsideration. If NP adopts the bill with a majority of two-thirds of its members, the law is promulgated within fifteen days.

If a motion of censure is adopted by the two thirds of deputies, the president should accept the resignation of his government. But if the same NP adopts a second motion of censure with a two-thirds majority during the same legislative period, the president of the republic may either accept the resignation of government or dissolve the NP by a decree. This decree has to include the calling for new elections within a maximum period of thirty days.

2. Economic System: Controlled Liberalism

Despite the non-democratic aspect of the Tunisian regime, the economic system is based on free market in general, while the state keeps control on some activities. Tunisia had made large steps towards liberalization, which contributed to strengthening growth performance, averaging 5.5 per cent per year since 1995 till 2000. Encouraged by more liberal exchange, trade and regulatory regimes, the private sector has expended rapidly in the export and tourism sectors, while domestic demands have been sustained by the rise of the real incomes of a large middle class.

Drought is still influencing economic performance especially that the agricultural sector is the most important. But Tunisia in 1990s made great performances in the sector of tourism sector. Government control of economic affairs, though still heavy, has gradually lessened over the past decade with increasing, simplification of tax structure. Tunisian association agreement with the European Union entered into force on March 1st,

1998. Under the agreement Tunisia will gradually remove barriers to trade with EU over the next decade (13).

The Tunisian government says that the legal environment of its economy is "characterized by its transparency, liberalism and efficiency. It is reflected in a favorable business law, reduced tariff barriers, a flexible tax system and simple and homogeneous rules for investment." Entered into force in January 1994, Investment Incentive Code (the law that governs both national and foreign investment) confirms the freedom to invest in most fields and reinforces the openness of the Tunisian economy to the global world. As a result, foreign direct investment flowed to Tunisia.

The privatization program for 2001 was to concern 41 public firms operating in various fields such as: industry, services, finance, tourism, trade, health and agriculture. The Tunisian Company for Hydrocarbons Transport by Pipeline "STRAPIL" announces floating shares of 30 per cent of the company's equities through the Tunisian stock market by launching a sale offer of 780.000 shares priced 12.500 Tunisian Dinars each.

Inflation has risen slightly, mainly because of higher food and petroleum prices. The same reason made external current account deficit (3.2 per cent of GDP in 2000) wider relative to 1999. The fiscal deficit had fallen in 2000 to around 3.5 per cent of GDP (excluding privatization grants), down from its 1999 level of 3.9 per cent of GDP.

Tunisian authorities' aim was to move to higher growth rate, consistent with a gradual reduction in the unemployment rate, which is too high, and with continued improvements in real wages and living standards. The macroeconomic framework reflecting these objectives envisages a progressive increase in real GDP growth to 6.7 per cent by 2006. About half of this growth would be close to 3.5 per cent per year and the fixed investment rate would rise from the current level of 26 per cent of GDP to 29 per cent of GDP by 2006, assuming an average annual increase of 80.000 people into the labor force. Always according to governmental sources, this scenario forecasts a drop in unemployment from 15.5 per cent in 2000 to 11 percent by 2006. Due to the restructure of the public banks, they could be protected against the systemic risks. IMF suggested more transparency, especially in the areas of accounting, financial reporting and enterprise ownership structures, as well as greater opening of the banking system to foreign investment (through privatization and equity participation). IMF considers that such actions would help improve and align bank and risk management practices to the requirements of a more open economy. Also, IMF suggests that inter-mediation should be developed through the capital markets, which continue to play a very marginal role in financing the economy in comparison with bank credit. The same international financial institution (IMF) recommends that Tunisia should:

- Continue the liberalization of the MFN regime in parallel with the process of trade liberalization with the European Union;

- Reform the insurance sector to help promoting institutional saving and thus will be an important factor in the development of capital markets especially financial inter-mediation, which should play a very important role in financing economy in comparison with the bank credit;

- Speed liberalization of the services sector which may help to provide significant boost of growth and investment (14).

3. Judicial System: Interference by the state

The international NGO "Transparency International" that fights against corruption classifies Tunisia in a good position. From time to time some employees are prosecuted in front of ordinary courts because of bribery, but the disease is still registered in the country (14).

There are no commercial courts in the Tunisian judicial system, and ordinary courts settle disputes of economic aspects. There are 110 courts: 1 high court, 8 courts of appeal, 23 courts of first instance, and 78 district courts.

The constitution considers the judiciary independent. Judgments are rendered in the name of the people and in the name of the president of the republic. The magistrates in the exercise of their functions are not subjected to any authority other than law. Magistrates are appointed by decree of the president of the republic upon recommendation of the Superior Council of the judges. This council watches over the application of the guarantees accorded to magistrates in the matter of nomination, advancement, transfer and discipline (16).

The high court is an important institution in any judicial system. The high court in Tunisia meets in a case of high treason committed by a member of the government. The competence and the composition of the high court are not clear in the constitution. The same for the council of state, which is, composed of two organs the administrative tribunal and the court of accounts. Organic laws, which were voted by parliament, and may be accepted or refused by the president, determine their composition and competence (ART. 28 and ART.52). This means that the majority determines them, and as a matter of fact, the president and government party RCD determines them.

On July 6th, 2001 the judge Mokhtar Yahyaoui addressed a message to the president of the republic saying that Tunisian justice is not independent and judges are forced by authorities to make decisions against the law and against their convictions. At the beginning, Yahyaoui was deprived of his salary, but after the Association of Judges, the Association of Lawyers, the Association of the Young Lawyers and many international NGOs supported him, all the sanctions taken against him were abolished (17).

---

(1) Modern History of Tunisia till 1987

(2) Conditions for candidacy to presidential elections

(3) MDS and Annahda outlawed

(4) Human rights activists consider democracy in Tunisia a right not a gift.

(5) If anyone wants to issue a publication in Tunisia he/she has to be permitted for that by the government.

(6) Treatment of human rights activists.

(7) Constitution of Tunisia, ART.8

(8) Ibid. ART. 23

(9) Ibid. ART. 26-2

(10) Ibid. ART. 28

(11) Ibid. ART. 40

(12) Ibid. ART. 40

(13) Economy-Tunisia-Association Agreement with the European Union

(14) IMF

(15) Transparency International—World Report 2000/Tunisia

(16) Constitution: Chapter of the judiciary.

(17) Jeune Afrique L'Inteligent, N° 2120—from 28 August till 3 September 2001, year 41.

-D-

LIBYA:
A REVOLUTION WITHOUT THE REVOLUTION

1. A Populist Democracy

Libya is an old constitutional state. Its first constitution was put into force in 1951. The second constitution was in 1961. But the *coup d'Etat* led by Mouamar Kaddafi in 1969 aborted the constitutional process. What is exceptional in the Libyan history is that this constitution was set before the independence. The constitution was promulgated on October 7th, 1951 and sovereignty was proclaimed on December 24th. This constitution was provided for a bicameral legislature (1). When Kaddafi and his young fellow officers overthrew King Idriss Senoussi and abolished the Libyan monarchy, the whole constitutional process was stopped forever. Before that, too near, on the east, Gamal Abdul Nasser proclaimed his revolution in Egypt against the west and all the "colonialist" ideas and monarchies.

A constitution and a state based on laws wasn't a question of that time. Revolutions in Europe (1700–1900) were based on constitutional projects. The uprisings that were storming against powerful monarchies were based on constitutional projects, and judicial innovations (2). In the Arab countries, the situation was different. There was a conflict between different social projects. Independents were declared also against "the colonialist" regimes inherited from real colonialism.

Liberal nationals were against socialist nationals. There were also those who were for a united Arab state based on Arab nationalism in Middle East and North Africa as a whole. This means that they were against state independence of Arab countries. This situation reflects how the major positions within the Arab elite were at that time (3).

The Libyan "Free Officers Movement," which stopped the constitutional process and claimed credit for carrying out the coup in 1969, met popular enthusiastic reception, especially by younger people in the urban areas, not only in Libya, but in nearly all other Arab countries. People didn't support the new regime, as they didn't have time to understand what it wanted to do, but just expressed their rejection for the king Idriss and his policy, and their support to Arab nationalism.

The constitution proclaimed by the defeated king wasn't prepared in a popular context. Limited elite around the royal family elaborated the constitution far away from the people. Therefore, when the *coup d'état* was launched at Benghazi, within two hours the takeover was completed. There was no resistance at all, and no deaths or violent incidents related to the coup were reported. This also means that the king was unpopular. His regime was characterized as belonging to "dark ages". The population supported the officers' revolt that was calling for prosperity, equality, and honor (4).

Influenced by the Palestinian-Israeli conflict, the Arab nation gave its total support to the Free Officers Movement. Many officers in other countries hoped to do the same, which encouraged Kaddafi to prepare his own political and ideological theory called "The Green Book". Published in 1976, the first book of "The Green Book" was about political systems and the theory on which "Aljamahiria" (6) was founded. This was declared on March 2nd, 1977. The second Green Book and the third one respectively about economic and society appeared in 1978 and 1979.

Kaddafi preaches that the political system he created is better than a democracy. He considers that democracy takes into consideration the majority and ignores minority, while his theory takes into account all people: both minority and majority at the same time (7). For this reason, Kaddafi created the Basic People's Congresses (BPC) where all adults have the right to participate in decision-making. Delegates of BPC are represented in the General People's Congress (GPC), a kind of national assembly that decides the guidelines of national politics (8).

Inside the GPC, there is no pluralism. Revolutionary ideology of the Green Book is the only one, which is tolerated. Citizens are considered revolutionaries by birth. If any one chooses other ways, he is considered a dissident.

For the Libyan authorities, western democracy is just a lie that covers dominance of hegemonic lobbies. Although many scholars say that democracy is only an alternative to political systems that existed before and it is maintained just because there is no other alternative (9). But the "Green Book" is far from being an alternative. It is just a populist version of communism. Political parties are outlawed. Freedom of expression isn't tolerated. The right to criticize political decision makers is out of consideration. So, how can we say that this political theory is, at least, equal to democracy?

Kaddafi tried to make a revolution in the old concept of the revolution as CHE Guevara did. But what Kaddafi did was just a political change, a revolution without the revolution. The essence of any revolution either political or ideological is to bring something completely new, if not to say the opposite. Capitalism was a revolution in Europe as it broke down feudalism and founded an economic system based on private single property. Capitalism had also revolutionized the production system from an economy based on agriculture to an economy based on industry. Socialism made property public, and assured the sharing of the surplus value by producers either in agriculture or industry. Kaddafi talked in his theory about sharing property, which isn't new if it is compared to socialism. In reality, property is put at last under the state's authority. This is what had happened in ex-socialist countries despite the glamorous theories about people's ownership of property.

Democracy was a revolution at its beginning. Its values and its methods in governing are still revolutionary ideas for any despotic regime. During the cold war period there was a "liberal democracy" and a "socialist democracy". The first was based on pluralism and direct secrete vote, while the second was built on the unique party and its supporters believe that democracy should be in economic rights, which means equality. They do not believe in political rights including the right to secret vote.

Kaddafi abolished the political parties. He considered them a medium to exploitation, but he made of the state as a whole one totalitarian party.

Before 1977, Kaddafi was governing his country according to the socialist model, a unique party the Arab Socialist Union (ASU), with a Pan Arab ideology. After September 1969's coup, the supreme organ of the revolution regime, the Revolutionary Council Committee (RCC), replaced the existing constitution with the Constitutional Proclamation of December 11th, 1969, which was to be superseded by a new constitution at some future, unspecified date. Meanwhile, existing laws, decrees and regulations not in conflict with the December proclamation remained in effect. The proclamation confirmed the RCC as the supreme authority of government. In 1971 RCC created ASU. Its intent was to raise the political consciousness of Libyans and aid the RCC in formulating public policy through debate in open forums. Trade unions were incorporated into the ASU, and strikes were forbidden. The press, already subject to censorship, was officially conscripted in 1972 as an agent to the revolution (10).

RCC's declared principle was to conduct the executive operation through a predominantly civilian cabinet of technician administrators. After the first *coup d'Etat* in December 1969, by Adam Said Hawwaz the minister of defense and Musa Ahmad the minister of interior, a new cabinet was formed. Kaddafi retained his post as chairman of the RCC and became prime minister and defense minister. Major Abdessalam Jallud, second to Kaddafi in the RCC, became deputy prime minister and minister of interior. In 1972, Jallud became prime minister in place of Kaddafi. Before that all routine administrative tasks fell to him. Two years later, he assumed Kaddafi's remaining administrative and protocol duties to "allow Kaddafi to devote his time to revolutionary theorizing," which was proved true when Kaddafi published the "Green Book" and started to restructure the Libyan society.

Beginning in early 1977, the new political order was clearly shaped in March when General People's Committee (GPC) adopted the "Declaration of the Establishment of the People's Authority" and proclaimed the Socialist People's Libyan Arab Aljamahiria (11).The GPC also adopted resolutions designating Kaddafi as its general secretary and creating the general secretariat of the GPC, comprising the remaining members of the defunct RCC. It also appointed the General People's Committee, which replaced the Council of Ministers, its members called secretaries rather than ministers. Both the legislative and executive authority was invested in GPC. This body delegated its authority to Kaddafi, its general secretary. This made Kaddafi the primary decision maker. But for Libyan leadership, the citizens' participation in discussion within local Basic People's Congress (BPC), whose decisions were passed up to the GPC for consideration and implementation as national policy, is the embodiment of what they termed "people's power." Revolutionary Committees, created in 1977, were assigned to the task of "absolute revolutionary supervision of people's power," which means that they were given the complete authority over Libyan citizens breaking the law. Both Basic People's Congresses and Revolutionary Committees assume in a way the same task, as they are directly related to people. This creates overlapping jurisdictions in which cooperation and coordination between these two elements are compromised.

Libya enjoyed the cold war period. Openly, it had supported many movements that were considered terrorist by western countries. But after the dissolution of the Soviet Union, Libyan international policy was unprotected. In 1986, American and British military bombers hit Libya and left behind many casualties including members of Kaddafi's family. Libya's complain to UN was in vain. Enjoying from his relations with many armed movements, Kaddafi proposed many times his mediation to solve some delicate problems such as the case of the seventeen hostages who were arrested by an Islamic movement (Abu Sayyaf) in the Philippines in August 2000. Once visited by the ex-Libyan ambassador in Manila, the rebels freed one of the hostages who were kidnapped with the 20 others on April 23rd, 2000. When a plane of passengers blasted over Lockerbie and left many casualties, two Libyan citizens were blamed. Kaddafi refused to hand them out to the American or Scottish justice. In 1992, the UN imposed a limited embargo to Libya. After 8 years, with the help of South African historical leader Nelson Mandela and other international personalities, it was convened that the two Libyans should be judged in an independent state: Netherlands. In January 2001, the court freed one Libyan, Alamin Fhima, and condemned Abdelbasit Mguarhi. In Tripoli,

Kaddafi said that the court's decision was political. Despite handing the accused citizens, the embargo went on. Many intellectuals in the region say that it is aimed to weaken Kaddafi's regime, but the result is totally the opposite. The result was the opposite: Kaddafi became stronger. Libyans discovered that western countries are "against the revolutionary choice of a nation."

Opposition to Kaddafi is the weakest in Arab countries. Largely supported by the United States, it has lost its credibility. From time to time international newspapers and international reports write about the students' rebellions, and soldiers' coup attempts. The regime treats all opponents harshly. They are considered renegades and western spies. Paralyzed by the regime's strength, the National Front for the Salvation of Libya (NFSL) that was founded in 1981 to "overthrow the Kaddafi regime, and to establish a national, democratic and constitutional alternative," couldn't prove credibility, and have any influence on Libyans (12).

After a long time of differences, the opposition gathered in Britain in 2005. The opposition activists called for a peaceful change and proposed to come back to 1951's constitution; urging Kaddafi to withdraw from power (!!). The call had no influence.

2. A Populist Policy led to A Populist Economy

The Populist policy of Kaddafi led him to a populist economy. The economic system is based on public property with the workers' participation in management. As a petroleum producer, with its limited population (7 Millions) the GDP is the highest in North African countries. Petroleum products accounted for between 50 and 60 per cent of GDP. Transportation and construction have accounted for relatively large shares. The large amount of development spending in agriculture was vain. The participation of the public service sector to GDP rose from 5 per cent in 1978 to 12 percent in 1984. The shortage of labor pushed private farms to hire lower paid foreign agricultural workers, mainly from Egypt.

"Radical measures put into effect in 1978 remained unclear in early 1987 reported an American research study. (13). The resolution-outlawing rental did increase the disposable incomes of renters, who in 1978 comprised an estimated one-third of the population. It also eliminated a major income source for landlords and removed what had been the main area of private investment. Although landlords were allowed to continue renting to those in need of short-term accommodation, the 1978 policies severely diminished the economic power of wealthy, large-scale property owners who had been a potent force in politics (14).

Law requiring worker participation in management has been less clear. In 1973 profit-sharing requirement probably increased the workers' incomes by requiring private and public firms to distribute one-quarter of their profits to workers. In 1978, when there was an extension of profit sharing, many owners liquidated their businesses rather than face their loss of control of them. Compared to pre-1969 Libya, there was a general rise in the standard of living for most people. This depends on stable oil revenues, when they start to fall; they begin to have tremendous effects on the Libyan economy.

For the banking system, the military government that took power in 1969 viewed the banking sector as a primary object of its general program of nationalization. In November 1969, the new government required that all banks in the country be Libyan controlled, and it bought out the 51 per cent control of the commercial banks that had not already converted to Libyan control. In July 1970, the government took 100 per cent control of four of the major banks with foreign minority ownership. In December 1970, the government purchased outright all banks that still had some foreign minority participation and, by a process of merging, reduced the number of commercial banks to five. In addition to the National Commerce Bank, commercial banks in operation in 1987 included the Aljama-hiria Bank, known as the Jumhuria (republic) Bank until 1977. Not only banks, insurance industry were also nationalized.

3. The Revolution Alone Represents The "Judicial" System

More than preaching for a new model in politics and economy, Kaddafi has his own judicial system. After the coup against the king Idriss, RCC was given the power to annul or reduce legal sentences by decree and declare general amnesties. The 1969 constitutional proclamation provided little guidance for the judiciary. Judges were independent except when political crimes were involved. It was reported that "after 1979, the situation deteriorated" (15).

In 1980, the Revolutionary Committees created the revolutionary courts. These courts formed a separate and parallel judicial system. Revolutionary committees established revolutionary courts that held public, often televised, trials of those charged with crimes against the revolution. In Libya there are no independent lawyers who can help those who are to be judged. A law promulgated in 1981, prohibited private legal practice and made lawyers employees of the Secretariat of Justice. Political courts were presided by RCC members. In 1971, a "People's Court" was established to try members of the former royal family and other officials. More than RCC members, this court was presided by one representative from the armed forces, the Islamic University, the Supreme Court and the police. Many "People's Courts" were hold for many opponents.

The court system has four levels:

First, the summary courts which are located in small towns. Each consists of a single judge who hears cases involving misdemeanors (disputes involving amounts up to 100 Libyan Dinars).

Second, the courts of first instance which hear appeals from summary courts and have original jurisdiction over all matters. It is formed of a panel of three judges who rule by majority decision; hear civil, criminal, and commercial cases.

Third, the appeal courts, which hear appeals from, first instance courts. Like courts of first instance, three judges rule by majority decision.

Finally, the Supreme Court, which comprises five chambers: civil and commercial, criminal, administrative, constitutional, and *sharia*. A five-judge panel sits in each chamber, and the majority shall establish the decision. The court is the final appellate body for cases emanating from lower courts. It can also interpret constitutional matters. However, it no longer has cassation or annulment power over the decisions of the lower courts, as it did before the 1969 revolution.

The Supreme Council of Judicial Authorities supervises courts. The same council establishes salaries and seniority rules for judges, whom it could transfer or retire. There is also the Council of State, which delivers advisory legal opinions for government bodies regarding draft legislation and other actions or regulations. It also includes an administrative court to provide relief in civil cases involving arbitrary or otherwise unfair administrative decisions.

---

(1) Most devoted Arab intellectuals who were devoted to struggle for freedom at the 60s and 70s weren't interested in constitutional democracy at all. What was the most important was to fight against imperialism and its values including "western democracy" that was based especially on pluralism.

(2) (e.g.) The French Revolution.

(3) Zartman, I. William. Political Elites and political development in the Middle East, New York: Schenkman, 1975.

(4) Bianco, Mirella. Kaddafi: Voice From the Desert, New York: Longman, 1975.

(5) Kaddafi, Mouamar al, The Green Book, Part I: The Solution of the problem of Democracy, London: Martin Brian and O'Keeffe, 1976.

(6) "Aljamahiria" was developed from the Arabic word "aljoumhouria" which means Republic. The difference between "Aljamahiria" and republic (according to the Green Book) is that in the first people govern themselves without state's institutions (with people's institutions), while in the second institutions "govern" people. The American scholar Lisa Anderson suggested "peopledom" to translate "Aljamahiria" which means the state

of the masses. For more details see: Libya: country study, ed: Congress Library, 1987, p39.

(7) Kadhafi talks about "direct democracy" which is "the basis of the political system in the socialist People's Libyan Arab Jamahiria, where the authority is in the hand of the people (March 2nd, 1977).

(8) See ICL. Libya—Declaration on the Establishment of the Authority of the People, ART.3 (2):

   The authority of the People is comprised of the following:

   People's congress;

   People's committees;

   Professional unions; and

   General People's Congress:

   The Libyan People is divided into basic People's Congresses

   All citizens register themselves as members of the Basic People's

   Congress in their area (...)

(9) Takashi Ingouchi, John Keane, and Edward Newman, editors, The Changing Nature of Democracy, UNU Series, 1999.

(10) See ICL—declaration (note No.8) The Preamble.

(11) Libye: Une Mediation de Connivence, Par Romain Franklin, in Liberation (newspaper) 17 August 2000.

(12) See: HYPERLINK http://www.nfsi-libya.com

(13) Libya. A country Study, American Congress Library.

(14) Ibid. Agriculture.

(15) See. Libya: From 1945 to 1980.

-E-

EGYPT:
THE OLDEST AND THE LATEST DEMOCRACY

1. Roots of Elected Bodies: At last an opposition

In June 1879, the law of the Deputies' Consultative Council (a primitive parliament) was passed in Egypt. In February 1882, the Constitution was promulgated holding the cabinet responsible before the representative house elected by the people for a five—year term. Although the cabinet was entitled to dissolve the council, it had the power of legislation and questioning ministers. In 1923, a new constitution was promulgated under the multi-party system (1). Despite this rooted democracy, in 2001 the one-party founded by Gamal Abdul Nasser took another name, but it was still dominating the political scene including the People's Assembly (parliament).

How that regression had happened in the Egyptian system?

On July 26th, 1952 King Faruk was forced to abdicate by Free Officers Movement led by Nasser (1), who had abrogated the constitution and dissolved parties. This movement started to govern the country through the Revolution Council Committee. In 1954, Nasser founded the Arab Socialist Party (ASP). It was officially the unique party that governed Egypt till 1977, when a new law regulating the establishment of political parties in Egypt, was issued (2).

The democratic process was hammered down by the "Socialist" regime of Nasser. The opposition was denied the right to free expression, and its members were tried for treason and jailed for very long periods (3). When the political parties came back according to Law number 40 regulating the establishment of political parties, the autocratic regime was dominating through its widespread elite. The opposition says that elections in Egypt are unfair, and the ruling party, the "National Democratic Party" (NDP) uses the state's authorities and capacities to keep his dominance (4).

Though the previous mentioned changes, Egypt is still a "presidential monarchy" where the president is elected for a six-year unlimited terms. The nomination to the post of President of the Republic used to be made in the People's Assembly upon the proposal of at least one third of its members. The candidate who wins two-thirds of the votes of the Assembly members was referred to the people for a plebiscite. The candidate was considered president of the republic when he obtained an absolute majority of the votes cast in the plebiscite. The President, who may be re-elected for an indefinite number of successive terms, may be charged of high treason or of committing a criminal act upon proposal by at least one-third of members of People's Assembly (Parliament). This accountability is scarce in third world countries where we find it either ambiguous or totally forgotten. The president appoints the Prime Minister, his deputies, the Ministers and their deputies and relieves them of their posts. He shall have the right to call and chair a meeting of the Council of Ministers. He shall also appoints the civil and military officials, and the diplomatic representatives, and dismiss them in the manner prescribed by the law. The president issues regulations for the implementation of laws and decisions for organizing the public services and interests.

These and other authorities of the president are traditional prerogatives since the 1952 revolution. Both Nasser and Mohamed Anouar Sadat were authoritarian presidents. Although the multi-party system was issued during his presidency of Egypt, Sadat was responsible for continuing Nasser's totalitarian regime based on the unique party system (5). Farouk regime that was considered by Free Officers Committee a regime that betrayed the nation assured pluralism and held the cabinet responsible before the parliament. Legally speaking, during his reign, there was an active political life despite that since 1950 until 1952; the Egyptian society was drawn in riots. After he declared the martial law, Muslim Brotherhood movement murdered Nuqrashi when he ordered them to dissolve themselves (6).

The popularity of any regime doesn't mean that it reflects people's natural will. Nasser's regime was popular because he represented a "courageous" regime against the "awkward" defeated one. But more than that, the RCC passed in 1952, shortly after the revolution, the Agrarian Reform

Law, which abolished the power of the absentee landlord class (7). Minimum wages were raised, working hours reduced, and state's investment in industry was encouraged, which created more jobs and unemployment problem was resolved. After this welcomed step within poor people and the middle class, political parties were abolished on January 17th, 1953.

With the help of the popular support, the unique party was founded. At the beginning it was named the Liberation Rally and served as an organization for the mobilization of popular support for the new government. After that, it was named the Arab Socialist Party, which is still dominating the political scene under its new name: the National Democratic Party (NDP). Despite the liberal choice of the state, the same party kept on its hegemonic position over the state and society. The Prime minister has forever been one of the leaders of the dominant party, and he always gets the confidence of parliament.

The PA may decide to withdraw its confidence from any of the prime minister's deputies after being questioned. Such motion should be proposed by one-tenth of the Assembly's members and pronounced by its majority, but it is not mentioned in the constitution if the prime minister and his cabinet as a whole may be forced to resign directly. The cabinet may be forced to resign after a long process through which the PA shall determine the responsibility of the Prime Minister and questioning him on a proposal made by one-tenth of the MPs. If the responsibility is proved, the parliament shall submit a report to the President of the Republic including the elements and conclusions reached on the matter and the reasons behind it. The President of the Republic may return such a report to the parliament within ten days. If the assembly ratifies it once again, the president may put the subject of discord to a referendum. If the result is in support of the government, the parliament should be considered dissolved, otherwise the president of the republic shall accept the resignation of the council of ministers. This authority, though too long in its procedure, reflects the extent to which the parliament controls the work of the executive. According to Article 86 of the constitution, the "people's Assembly shall exercise the legislative power and approve the general pol-

icy of the State, the general plan of economic and social development and
the general budget of the state."

The very bad remark that undermines the independence of the legislative authority (PA) is that the president who represents the executive body
may "appoint a number of members." Even if it does not exceed ten, as a
constitutional obligation, it may help the president to influence the parliament's work at least by asking questions or revealing subjects after being
consulted by the President of the Republic.

In 1995, President Husni Mubarak appointed Khalid Muhi-eddin to
be member of the parliament. Muhi-eddin is a famous opposition leader
known by his high moral integrity. He was a member of Free Officers
Movement, which had thrown the King Farouk. Muhi-eddin who was
head of the main and most credible opposition party, refused to seat in
parliament after this nomination by the president. Muhi-eddin was
defeated in what he considered falsified elections. Some intellectuals who
support Husni Mubarak say that this constitutional possibility enables the
president to create such equilibrium. If the opposition doesn't get any seat,
they say, he may make it represented to express its views in parliament.
But the opposition says that this is just a way to overturn falsification (8).

Despite the true allegations about the unfair elections, the official opposition is still weak. The Islamists are stronger. In November 2000's elections they got 17 seats. They were presented as independent candidates.
The weakness of the official opposition is due to its historical links with
the authority. During Nasser and Sadat's early years rule, they were part of
the governing elite. When separated, they couldn't cope alone. The Islamists who were the real opposition of past decades went on being the most
influent political branch within people.

Instead of encouraging moderate Islamists who chose to participate in
elections, the Egyptian government sued them of belonging to a banned
political movement (Muslim Brotherhood that was outlawed by Nasser in
February 1954, the next month of his access to power) (9). As the "official" opposition got weaker the legislative institution gets less important in
political life. This is true for Egypt. Constitutional prerogatives of parlia-

ment are very important, but the general activity of the institution doesn't attract people sufficiently, which puts the main opposition outside parliament, outside the general politics of the state. This political behavior encourages radicalism within extremist groups. While a participative approach may have helped to change the methods and positions of the opposition, the government did nothing, and the Islamic movement is actually an opposition to the state as a whole. If participation is made possible to its members, they may become like any opposition to any government. Once the way is open to participate in government, they may be ministers, which may convince them of the importance of a constructive opposition. Surely, this choice may undermine the effect of violent groups especially that it is—in theory—possible to act from inside government. But when the regime is undemocratic and there is no political transparency, it is scared of the opposition because it may make them accountable for their acts when they were in government.

When Mubarek tried to show openness towards the opposition after internal and international pressures, and proposed the amendment of the constitution to open presidential elections to many candidates, the major opposition force called for a boycott of the referendum. Ayman Nour the leader of AL-Ghad (tomorrow) Parti, the activist and scholar Saâd Eddin Ibrahim, and the writer Nawal Saâdaoui were at the origin of the large movement that called for change.

When he declared himself candidate for the fifth term, Mubarek is making a huge risk. The popular Egyptian Movement for change, the coalition of liberals and Islamists known as "Kifaya" (enough) may not give up the fight to make an end to the president's decades in power. The traditional opposition parties such as the liberal Wafd, the National Nasserist Party, and the leftist "Tagamou Parti" may be on "Kifaya" side.

The presidential elections reemphasized Mubarek at his seat, but the legislative elections brought a remarkable change. The banned Muslim Brotherhood, whose candidates stood independents, won 88 seats. The National Democratic Party of Mubarek lost 83 seats. In 2000 it gained 404 seats.

The new Islamic opposition may strengthen the legislative power. Though, the political sphere is still a handicap for applying democracy to the architecture of the whole system. The constitution makes the legislative authority totally invested in People's Assembly (parliament). According to the constitution, the parliament shall exercise the legislative power and approve the general policy of the state (10). Every member of the PA has the right to propose laws. After being ratified by PA, draft laws may be objected to by the President of the Republic. In this case, he has to send the draft law back to the PA within thirty days. If the draft is not sent back within this period, it is considered a law and shall be promulgated. But if it is sent back to the Assembly on the said date and approved once again by a majority of two-thirds of the members, it is also considered a law and shall be promulgated.

The PA has the power to form an ad hoc committee or entrust any of its committees with the inspection of the activities of any administrative departments, or the general establishments, or any administrative or executive organ. Its purpose is to find facts and inform the Assembly as to the actual or administrative, or economic positions, or for conducting investigations into a subject related to one of the said activities.

Also, PA is entitled to discuss the president's statement before the Assembly, and the prime minister's program. The President hasn't the right to dissolve parliament unless a referendum of the people is held. The decision to dissolve parliament shall comprise an invitation to electors to conduct new elections within a period not more than sixty days from the date of the declaration of the results of the referendum results. The new parliament shall convene during a period of ten days following the completion of elections.

PA approves the general plan for economic and social development. The final account of the State budget shall be submitted to the people's Assembly within a period not exceeding one year from the date of the expiration of the fiscal year (12). Accountability of ministries is one medium to improve economy and this is one step between others including what President Husni Mubarak calls his main project: *"Infitah"* (openness). As vice-president, Mubarak inherited in 1981 power on the basis of constitutional legitimacy at Sadat's death. He consolidated Sadat's limited political liberalization and maintained the major lines of Sadat's policies while trying to overcome some of their excesses and costs (13).

2. Economy: Out of the Totalitarian System

Since 1981, Mubarak has been trying to draw Egyptian economy out of totalitarianism where the public sector is hegemonic. Banking had fallen, also, under the government's control during the Nasser era. Banks were nationalized in 1963. They were four: the National Bank of Egypt, the Bank of Alexandria, Bank Misr, and the Bank of Cairo. They were owned and regulated by the Central Bank. Numerous special-purpose banks were created, including those for industrial and agricultural credit, mortgages, and social security funds. They had about 9 percent of total assets of banking system.

Under Sadat's rule, a law (Number 43 of 1974) for Arab and Foreign Capital Investment and Free Zones was extended to the domestic private sector. Banking boomed and its structure was altered. The number of banks grew between 1974 and 1988 from 8 to more than 100.

The Congress Library Country Study about Egypt stated, "Good performance of the banking sector was marred by corruption, embezzlement, smuggling of hard currency abroad, and a stormy confrontation between the government and the Islamic investment companies."

Islamic investment companies came into being in 1984 and were dominated by major firms, which grew accumulated, deposits totaling billions of dollars. Their practices differed from those of other banks in that they offered depositors risky open-ended mutual fund certificates instead of interest, which they say that Islamic law forbids as "usury." Initially, they were able to offer depositors returns of 20 percent. The government accused them of being able to do so through black-market money trading and by luring depositors with "pyramid" schemes, such as the establishment of fictitious corporations, by which dividends were paid from old investment. They were also charged with smuggling large sums of hard currency abroad and with defrauding many depositors. In 1988, the government issued new regulations that required the companies to reconstitute themselves as stock holding enterprises, issue share certificates, and place deposits under official scrutiny. The state's intervention made that interest rates remain the same through the 1980s. They were ranged from 5 to 15 percent for deposits and 11 per cent for loans.

Although most of the Arab students learnt that agriculture started in Egypt (in the Nile Delta), actually drought made that farming in Egypt was confined to less than 3 percent of the total land area. More than that, when the state implemented land reform programs, as in the socialist regimes, confusion was huge between collective property and state's intervention, which made farmers, became state employees at the end. Under Mubarak's rule state's control was relaxed, and private sector methods were encouraged. Although farmer workers are the poorest social class, in 1988 agriculture contributed more than 20 per cent of GDP and about 9 per cent of exports and employed more than one-third of total employment. In 1999, it was lowered to 17 per cent, but its capacity of employment was maintained to 40 per cent.

Industry includes energy, mining, and manufacturing. It shares about 33 per cent of GDP. However, the sector did not perform as well as in other aspects, especially in the creation of employment.

Services are the backbone of the Egyptian economy. Based on tourism, they share 51 per cent of GDP with 38 of labor force. For this reason, terrorism is a great danger; especially that it is directed towards tourists.

The participation in the Gulf war coalition helped Egypt to erase external debt. Coupled with IMF arrangement and structural reforms such as privatization and new business legislation, the general economic situation improved. Ten years after, and despite these improvements, the macroeconomic situation was far from reassuring IMF experts who judge economic reforms important, but very slow (15).

Although the liberalization of the economy is going forward, the constitution still stipulates that "The Arab Republic of Egypt is a democratic, socialist State based on the alliance of working forces of the people" (16).

The same is for the judicial system where we find that the institution of "The Socialist Public Prosecutor" is still responsible for "taking the procedure which (...) [preserve] the socialist achievements, and commitment to the socialist behavior."

3. Judicial System: Fairness and Strength

In spite of the above clause that has no significance in real life, the Egyptian judiciary system is the strongest and the most independent in Arab countries. This is due especially to the bar association and the experienced judges. In 1984, courts overturned a ban on the Wafd Party, threw out the Electoral law of 1984, and declared unconstitutional a Sadat decree issued in the absence of parliament. Judges expanded the scope of the freedom of the press by dismissing libel suits of government ministers against the opposition press and widened the scope of labor rights by dismissing charges against the strikers.

Serious human rights reports recognize that the judiciary body is independent in Egypt as it is mentioned in the constitution. It also provides for the independence and immunity of judges and forbids any interference by other authorities in the exercise of their judicial functions.

The president appoints all judges upon recommendation of the High Judicial Council: a constitutional body composed of senior judges, and chaired by the President of the Supreme Court of Appeal *(F. Cour de cassation)*. The council regulates judicial promotions and transfers. There are three levels of regular criminal courts: Primary courts, courts of appeal, and the Supreme Court of appeal; the final stage of criminal appeal. The judicial system is based on the Napoleonic tradition; hence, there are no juries. Misdemeanors that are punishable by imprisonment or fines are heard at the first level by one judge; at the second level by three judges. Felonies that are punishable by imprisonment or execution are heard in criminal court by three judges. The Supreme Court of Appeal hears contestation of rulings.

Military and State Security Emergency Courts state on political crimes, and don't guarantee fair trial. Human right activists in Egypt call for the abolition of these courts. Another specific court is the "Court of Ethics." It was created in 1980 as a separate judicial institution to investigate complaints of widespread corruption and illegal business practices. The Office of the Socialist Prosecutor served as watchdog against abuses by government officials, approved the credentials of candidates for office in the trade union movement, professional syndicates, and local government councils, and performed security checks on senior government appointees.

Although the Egyptian legal system is built on *sharia* (Islamic law), the court system is chiefly secular. It applies criminal and civil law deriving primarily from the French heritage. Muslim political activists fought successfully and achieved the passage of a constitutional amendment making the *sharia* in principal the unique source of legislation, a potential ground for ruling unconstitutional a whole corpus of secular law. More than this, and according to *sharia*, an Egyptian court stated that the writer Nasser Hamid Abouzid was married unlawfully to his wife after writing what it was considered secular books (17).

---

(1) Deeb, Marius. Party Politics in Egypt: The Wafd and Its Rivals, 1919–1939. London. Ithaca Press, 1979.

See also: Hunter, Robert. Egypt under the Khedives, 1805–1879: From Household Government to Modern Bureaucracy. Pittsburg: University of Pittsburgh, 1984.

(2) Hopwood, Derek. Egypt: Politics and society, 1945–1984. Boston. Allen and Unwin, 1985.

(3) Ibrahim, Ibrahim. 2 Religion and politics under Nasser and Sadat, 1952–1981, in Barbara Freyer stowasser (ed.9 The Islamic Impulse (pp 121-134), London: croom Helm, 1987.

(4) Alahrar most of the time represent the extremist positions

(5) Mcdermott, Anthony. Egypt from Nasser to Mubarak: A Flawed Revolution. London: Croom Helm, 1988.

(6) Vatikiotis, P.J. The History of Egypt from Muhammad Ali to Sadat. Baltimore: Johns Hopkings University Press, 1980.

(7) Saab, Gabriel. The Egyptian Agrarian Reform, 1952–1962. London: Oxford University Press, 1967.

(8) The supporting newspaper to government is "ALAHRAM" that dedicates its editorials to the defence of the government's views.

(9) Dekmejian, Richard Hrair. Egypt Under Nasir: A study in Political dynamics. Albany: State University of New York Press, 1971.

(10) The constitution, ART. 86 (Chapter II: The Legislature).

(11) Ibid. The President ART. 130-131

(12) Ibid. ART 114-118.

(13) Harik, Iliya. Continuity and change in Local Development policies in Egypt, International Journal of Middle East Studies, 16, No.1, 1984, pp 13-66.

(14) IMF. Country Study

(15) Egypt: A Country Study, Library of the Congress.

(16) The Constitution, the Preamble.

(17) Amnesty international annual report 1999.

VI. *Human Rights In North African Countries*

INTRODUCTION: THE CULTURAL AND THE POLITICAL CONTEXT

When the Universal Declaration of Human Rights (UDHR) was adopted in the early morning of 10 December 1948, most of the North African countries were not independent. Only Egypt was. More than that, it was member of the drafting committee of UDHR with Lebanon. These were the only two Arab countries represented, and they were in the position of influencing the draft of the declaration by including some "Arab cultural values."

Unfortunately Egypt's representative Omar Lofti wasn't active at all. But representative of Lebanon Charles Malik could influence the whole debate. He was the reporter of the drafting commission.

After the independence of the last colonized country (Algeria in 1961) North African Countries (NAC) were able to participate in more than one draft of the basic International Instruments.

The International Convention on Economic, social, and cultural Rights and the International Covenant on Civil, and Political Rights were adopted by the UN General Assembly on 16 December 1966. NAC could have participated in the drafting of these two major international instruments, but the "participation" came in different dates during ratification when they had included many reserves (!!)

Reserves are permitted in international law while ratifying any convention. But reserves shouldn't be to the main principles on which the same convention is based. Unfortunately the expression of the "main principles" is not clearly defined. Some countries made reservation in Convention of the Elimination of all sorts of Discrimination Against Women to the right of women to dissolve marriage. The man may have this right, and he may use it without his wife's consent or even knowing about that. Today, many domestic legal systems in the world, consider as a kind of rape forcing a woman to go on living at wedlock.

Most of the Islamic countries, including NAC, advance the interpretation of some Koranic verses, which is controversial, and many scholars say that women has not the absolute right to divorce. It is the same for catholics who prohibit divorce for both the man and the woman. The European Court of human Rights decided that there is violation of Art.8 of the European Convention for the Protection of Human Rights and Fundamental Freedoms in the interest of a catholic woman, which means that the right of dissolution of marriage should be preserved. The opposite is a violation of human rights. So, domestic laws should preserve this fundamental right, but this is not the case in some NAC as we will see later.

During cold war period, human rights were subject to challenge between East and West. Algeria and Libya were by the East side, while Morocco, Tunisia, and Egypt (since late seventies) were by the West. But all of them had very bad human rights records. Though they were different in their domestic legislation, the political reality was nearly the same; no multy-party system, no freedom of expression and right to hold opinion, and no right to association. At the same time there were many political detainees, cases of disappearances, and sometimes political killings, which made that the whole region underwent dark decades.

The absence of democracy was the origin of all that. Shortly after the independence, the political movements were faced after their first day of independence by "the masters of the new colonisation." These were those who used to share with them the hope and the wish for an independent, democratic, and prosperous country. Backed by the ex-colonising states, the new elite in power started a bloody confrontation against all those who had dared to oppose. In Algeria, Houari Boumedien declared bloody war against his "red" fellows, and ended by putting in jail "white" ones (liberals) including the first president of the state Ahmed Benbella. In Tunisia,

Habib Bourguiba outlawed opposition and most of its leaders were either jailed or exiled.

National movements used to gather all the forces of the nation to overthrow colonial powers and send their soldiers back to their countries of origin. All political tendencies were belonging to the same broad movement. The leader was the man who could gather people behind him, and incite his co-citizens to make the revolution. This man was that one who went to dialogue with the occupation authorities after they were weaken by people's struggle. Many political leaders of the time didn't agree totally or partly about how independence was reached, so they went to opposition in the aftermath of independence, while their fellows went to power.

The two sides were very strong that confrontation between the two parts left many victims behind. As those who got power were those who won, jails were fall of the liberation fellows. This was dramatic. Political prosecution based on ideological differences was a North African phenomenon of the post colonial period.

If it was a weak opposition, there shouldn't have been thousands of human rights victims. The opposition was strong. Its aim was to throw governments. This urged governments to cling more and more to power. Some times under the fear of being thrown, sometimes with clear political will, they used to shoot at all those who dared to say "No" to their policies.

When they were asked either by their fellow citizens or by foreigners about the respect of human rights, they were delighted to say that they are sovereign, meaning that they have the right to do whatever they want in their country.

A. SOVEREIGNTY: NO SHADE FOR VIOLATORS

The doctrine of sovereignty was developed as part of the transformation of medieval system in Europe into the modern state system, a process that culminated in the Treaty of Westphalia in 1648. Internationally, sovereignty served as the basis for exchanges of recognition on the basis of legal equality, and therefore as the basis of diplomacy and international law (1). This is called in political theory "external sovereignty," that opposes "internal sovereignty" which lies in the supreme command over "a civil society (2)," and it has a *de jure* (legal) aspect, as well as a *de facto* (coercive) aspect. Legal sovereignty vests in that person, office or body whose decisions can not legally be challenged in the court (!!) Coercive sovereignty vests in that person, office or body which in fact controls the powers exerted and enforced in name of government. William Blackstone (1723–1780) wrote in "Commentaries on the Laws of England 1765–1770" that "there is and must be in every state a supreme, irresistable, and uncontrolled authority, in which the right of sovereignty resides (3)."

"Uncontrolled authority." This is the shade that many rulers retained from the whole determination of sovereignty, because they found it fitting their interests and able to cover their acts. By the time and historical evolution, internal control mechanisms were set, but external ones that make governments accountable in front of international community about their internal polities is a new phenomenon that is still at the start of the third millennium raising highly controversial discussions. States access to international human rights treaties made States Parties accountable in front of the commissions prescribed by the same conventions. Reporting systems make the committees able to address observations about governments' violations and implementation of treaties' provisions. Even if NAC ratified many International Instruments, they went on saying till recent years that human rights are internal matters (4).

Since 1948, UDHR made it clear that "human rights should be protected by the rule of law" and "Everyone is entitled to all the rights and freedoms (…) without discrimination of any kind, such as race, color, sex, language, religion, political or other opinion, national or social origin, property, birth or other status (5)." Thus, it was made clear that "everyone's" rights should be protected, and more than this, the declaration guaranteed many rights that are clearly related to domestic laws and political practices; such as protection against torture, effective remedy for acts violating fundamental rights, and protection against arbitrary arrest, detention or exile.

Since then, It was clear that sovereignty of states over people started to take another meaning by which the state should protect citizens. The evolution of international instruments made it clear that the old meaning of sovereignty is senseless. On 16 December 1966, the General Assembly of the United Nations adopted and opened for signature, ratification and accession a revolutionary instrument. It is the Optional Protocol to the International Covenant on Civil and Political Rights (OP-ICCPR). It states that the Human Rights Committee on Civil and Political Rights (called the Committee) has the authority to "receive and consider communications from individuals (…) who claim to be victims of violations of any of the rights set forth in the covenant (6)." Although the OP-ICCPR provided that victims should exhaust "all available domestic remedies (7)" before submitting a written communication to the Committee for consideration, this was an enormous step, a revolutionary one, as it allows the international community to monitor relations between the state and its subjects.

The importance of this mechanism lays in its moral value. The whole process ends by the committee's view forwarded to the State Party concerned and to the individual, after holding close meeting when examining communications under the OP-ICCPR.

Also, states' reporting is important. The Committee's concluding remarks about States Parties reports regarding the implementation of the rights referred to in the ICCPR. The Committee is tolerated to use just these "soft" measures, as the use of force is limited in international law to an international intervention after decision by the security council, or whenever a state acts in self defense.

Bernard Couchner called for an immediate and systematic intervention if human rights are violated regardless of "sovereignty," or anything else. The world is still reticent about the "how and when" of the whole idea. What makes an intervention in favor of human rights, and what makes it an aggression? This is the question.

Kenneth Roth, executive director of Human Rights Watch (HRW), said that humanity will "remember 1999 as the year in which sovereignty gave way in places where crimes against humanity were being committed (…) Ordinarily we depend on sovereign States to defend human rights. But sovereignty can not be used as an excuse to avoid human rights commitments." While presenting HRW world report 2000, Roth regretted the "need for military force" to defend human rights, but praised the "decision to overrule the claims of tyrants and war criminals to be protected by the cloak of national sovereignty." At the same time, he noted that "governments using military force in the name of human rights should be subjected to close scrutiny, both for the methods they use in warfare, and the objectives they pursue."

B. Women: The Forgotten Half

The equal rights of men and women revealed cultural and religious differences within the drafting commission of the UDHR. Family and marriage raised divergent views. Right to marry and to found a family "had not been foreseen as part of the declaration." At that moment the term "full age" in article16 (1) was opposed by some Muslim countries which suggested reference to law (8).

Mexico proposed that men and women "should enjoy the right to marry and found a family without any limitation due to race, nationality and religion." Though a Muslim country, Egypt voted for this proposal while Saudi Arabia abstained. This was rejected because many countries, including the western considered it merely a "restatement of the content of article 2 of the UDHR." Charle Malik proposed to add "free and" before the words "full consent" in paragraph 2 to be "Marriage shall be entered into only with the free and full consent of the intending spouses."

Right to marry implies "obligations for the State. First, it creates an obligation for the state to protect the right to marry against the interference of third parties (private). Second, it implies that the state has to provide for marriage as an institution law"(9).

In NAC marriage is institutionalized in private law, but the same law used to give parents (third parties) in these countries the right to refuse marriage of a woman to a man she had chosen. Since October 10th, 2003

big changed happened in Morocco first. The King Mohammed VI has
proposed advanced reforms including the right to men and women at full
age to marry themselves without the parents' consent. Parents' consent to
their daughter's marriage was a *senni qua non* obligation. But men are free
to marry who ever they want. More than this, they may marry four wives
at the same time, and women have not the right to divorce, or to marry a
second man. From the human rights point of view, there "may be temporary prohibitions on the marriage of women, in order to protect the interests of the child to be born, and on the father in case the woman should be
pregnant (10)."

In Islam divorced women has the right to marry only three months after
the day of her divorce. It is considered for the interest of the child, especially to know who is his/her father. This law supposes that the woman
may be pregnant. Laws do not foresee that women shall have the right to
marry if medical tests prove that she is not pregnan. Although the woman
may be pregnant, her ex-husband may be married.

After the UDHR, the international community adopted many conventions on women's rights. On 7 November 1967, the General Assembly
(GA) of the UN proclaimed the Convention on the Elimination of all
sorts of Discrimination Against Women (CEDAW), which states in its
first article that "discrimination against women, denying or limiting as it
does their equality of rights with men, is fundamentally unjust and consti-
tutes an offence against human dignity." The same declaration urged states
to take all appropriate measures to ensure women's right to "vote in all
elections and be eligible" and the right to "hold public office." After that,
the GA adopted on 18 December 1979, the Convention on the Elimination of All sorts of Discrimination Against Women (CEDAW). This convention defined "discrimination against women" as "any exclusion or
restriction made on the basis of sex which has the effect or purpose of
impairing or nullifying the recognition, enjoyment or exercise by women,
irrespective of their marital status, on a basis of equality of men and
women, of human rights and fundamental freedoms in the political, economic, social, cultural, civil or any other field." Through the same conven-

tion that entered into force on 3 September 1981 in accordance with article 27(1), States Parties "condemn discrimination against women in all its forms [and] agree to pursue by all appropriate means and without delay a policy of eliminating discrimination against women." Also, the convention urged states to take "all appropriate measures" to change and modify the "social and cultural patterns of conduct of men and women, with a view to achieving the elimination of prejudices and customary and all other practices which are based on the idea of inferiority or the superiority of either of sexes or on stereotyped roles for men and women" ART.5(a). Article 18 provided that "States Parties undertake to subdue to the Secretary-General of the United Nations, for consideration by the Committee [on the Elimination of all sorts of Discrimination Against Women], a report on the legislative, judicial, administrative or other measures which they have adopted to give effect to the provisions of the present convention (CEDAW) and on the progress made in this respect."

For marriage, CEDAW emphasized on equality and freedom during marriage as the basis for union and disunion between men and women. Article 16 urged states to "take appropriate measures to eliminate discrimination against women in all matters relating to marriage and family relations." This means *inter alia* the right to enter into marriage freely or to its dissolution, and the same rights and responsibilities with regard to guardianship, ward-ship, trusteeship and adoption of children. Also, the same rights for both spouses in respect of the ownership, acquisition, management, administration, enjoyment and disposition of property, whether free of charge or for a valuable consideration.

North African Countries registered their reservations to many articles in the above mentioned convention, including some main articles. CEDAW and all other treaty bodies of the United Nations declare that reservation "incompatible with the object and purpose of the present convention (CEDAW) shall not be permitted" ART.28(2). This matter rises great discussions while dealing with states' reports within this committee.

Five years before CEDAW, the International Covenant on Civil and Political Rights (ICCPR) had already entered into force (23 March 1976). Adopted on 16 December 1966, ICCPR provided that the States Parties should "ensure the equal right of men and women to the enjoyment of all civil and political rights."

C. CIVIL AND POLITICAL RIGHTS: DAILY ABUSE

Civil and political rights were in NAC subject to severe violations. Governments were not freely elected. They were either military regimes (Algeria, Libya, and Egypt) or absolutist nationalists (Morocco, and Tunisia). Opposition leaders were jailed without fair trials, demonstrators were shot to death, freedom of expression and association was far of being reached, and torture was practiced. In spite of these practices, states ratified the ICCPR. Like many other Third world countries, they were considering both signature and ratification a formal step. They were very late in submitting their critical reports. But with the help of internal struggle, the international community influence, and the growing importance of human rights in the international scene, NAC started to take human rights more seriously, and gave up to hide behind sovereignty, and cultural and religious specific features.

1. Morocco: Out of Dark

In its comments after consideration of Morocco's third report on civil and political rights (November 1999), the Committee on Civil and Political Rights concluded that "there is no agency fully independent of government with general responsibility for monitoring the implementation of human rights." Though the lack of independence the Justice and Reconciliationn Commission (IER), a body created in Junuary 2004 to deal with human abuses that occurred between 1956 and 1999, could organize public hearing in many cities, where victims were able to talk about their endurance. The first hearing was brodcasted live on the national TV station.

Some of the IER's prerogatives was to find the truth about disappeared persons and individual and collective abuses to determine indemnities.

IER made recommendations in its final report that was supposed to be submitted to the parliament, political parties, trade unions and human rights associations to debate it and enhance a reconciliation culture. Though some moroccan NGOs criticized the IER bitterly for not naming those who were responsible for torture and massive human abuses, the work done by this body was remarkable; especially discovering collective tombs of victims.

There's a lot to be done to promote the rule of law and promoting democracy and human rights culture. The above mentioned Committee concluded by the same occasion that:

1. The high rate of female illiteracy underlines the lack of equal opportunity for women in all aspects of society, and there is a discrimination against women in education, employment, public life and criminal and civil laws, including laws dealing with inheritance, marriage, divorce, family relations (polygamy, repudiation of marriage, grounds for divorce, age of marriage and restrictions on marriage by muslim women to non-muslims).

2. The maternal mortality due to clandestine, unsafe abortion because of strict prohibition on abortion, even in cases of rape or incest, and the stigmatization of women who give birth to children outside marriage.

3. There are no special program, legal sanctions or protective measures to counter violence and sexual abuse of women, including marital rape, and that there are aspects off the criminal law (such as crime of honor defense) which fail to provide equal protection of women's rights.

4. There were many cases of disappeared persons in Morocco, and there was no investigation about the responsibility for these disappearances.

5. These are allegations of torture and ill-treatment practiced by police officials, and these have been dealt with, if at all, only by

disciplinary measures and not by the imposition of criminal sanctions on those responsible for such violations.

6. The maximum length of detention of a suspect before being
    brought before a judge may in some cases be as 96 hours, and pre-
    trial detention is too long.

7. Fair trial guarantees, such as presumption of innocence and the
    right to appeal in criminal cases, are not fully reflected in the con-
    stitution or in the Code of Criminal Procedure. Also, there is no
    review by higher courts of decisions handed down by special
    courts like the Permanent Court of the Royal Armed Forces and
    the Special Court of Justice.

8. Freedom of religion and belief is not fully guaranteed. And free-
    dom of expression is restricted, and seizure of publication is pro-
    vided by law. Also, the requirement of a receipt of notification of
    an assembly is often abused. The committee recommended that
    notification should be required to outdoor assemblies and proce-
    dures should be adopted to ensure the issue of a receipt in all
    cases.

In 2001, NGOs' annual reports were less severe than they were before.
The appointment of Mr. Abderahman Youssoufi as a Prime Minister in
1998 was welcomed all over the world. He was exiled from 1962 till 1975.
In 1988, he became the First Secretary of the traditional socialist opposition party (USFP). Some Father Founders of Moroccan human rights
NGOs were appointed ministers within the same cabinet. This had happened for the first time in Moroccan history. Till 1998, cabinets were
headed by state's officials. Under the rule of Youssoufi's cabinet the King
Hassan II freed the remained political detainees after a similar decisions
taken in 1994.

Mohammed VI accession to the thrown after his father's death in July
1999, and his clear determination to respect and promote human rights
was appreciated by widely known international human rights NGOs. In
its annual reports 2000, Amnesty International (AI) wrote that: "Follow-

ing his enthronement, King Mohammed VI spoke about the importance of human rights, including women's rights. In November he replaced Interior Minister Driss Basri who had held this position since 1979." During the second month of his reign, Mohammed VI established an arbitration body to decide on compensation for the victims of disappearances and arbitrary detention. This body received 5127 claims by the end of December 1999. On 21 June 2001, this body declared that it had already agreed to compensate 376 cases.

The Moroccan government says that "there are no political detainees in jails." But AI said that in 2001, there were five prisoners of conscience. Mohammed Dadach was blaimed of trying to escape from the army towards Polisario camps. Brahim Laghzal, Cheikh Khaya, and Laarbi Massoudi were sentenced to prison by the Court of Appeal in Agadir (south) for "threatening state security." Mustapha Adib Transparency International prize winner, was sentenced to imprisonment by the Military Court of Rabat and dismissed from the armed forces for indiscipline and dishonoring the army, after he published an article in *"Le Monde"*, denouncing corruption in the army.

An official human rights institution, exceptional of its kind, was founded in December 1993 by the King Hassan II. It is the Ministry of Human Rights with a minister member of the cabinet at its head, appointed by the king. At that time the Moroccan human rights' record was very dark. It was meant to express to the world that Morocco has no problem with human rights. The ministry's constitution states clearly that this establishment should receive complaints, promote human rights through education, incorporate international conventions ratified by the country in domestic law, and be responsible for international human rights relations of the kingdom. By natural evolution, this ministry became a real institution of human rights. By its work, all those who were suspicious at the beginning, were sure that it could participate effectively in the promotion and protection of human rights. Most of the Arab NGOs, including the Arab Organization of Human Rights (AOHR), called other Arab Countries to institute a ministry of human rights. Recently, the Republic of Yemen had its own and the same for Iraq.

Morocco had submitted its fifth periodic report to the Human Rights Committee in October 2004. The concluding observations of the Committee (CCPR/CO/82/MAR. Morocco. 01/12/2004) were as follows:

1. The Committee noted with appreciation that since the submission of its fourth periodic report (CCPR/C/115/Add.1), Morocco has pursued democratic reforms, adopted legislation in this regard (including the new Family Code) and created the office of Ombudsman (Diwan Al Madhalim).

2. The Committee welcomed the State party's commitment to pursuing the reforms with a view to fully implementing the rights set forth in the Covenant and its intention to accede to the Optional Protocol to the Covenant.

3. The Committee welcomes the State party's practice, which it has followed consistently since 1994, of commuting death sentences.

4. The Committee welcomes the decision of 26 September 2000 by Morocco's Supreme Court concerning the primacy of article 11 of the Covenant, prohibiting imprisonment for inability to fulfil a contractual obligation, over domestic law and practice. It notes with interest the content of the letter dated 7 April 2003 referring to the above-mentioned Supreme Court decision, in which the Minister of Justice requests the principal public prosecutors at appeal courts and courts of first instance to apply article 11 of the Covenant and to refer back to the courts the cases of all persons serving such sentences.

5. The Committee notes with appreciation that there is an advanced network of non-governmental human rights organizations in Morocco.

The principal subjects of concern and recommendations of the Committee were:

1. The Committee expressed concerns about the lack of progress on the question of the realization of the right to self-determination

for the people of Western Sahara (Covenant, art. 1). The committee urged the State party to make every effort to permit the population groups concerned to enjoy fully the rights recognized by the Covenant.

2. The Committee regretted the lack of specific information on the dealings of the Ombudsman (Diwan Al Madhalim) with the Administration. The requested the State party to supply statistical data on the work of the Ombudsman.

3. The Committee expressed concerns that Moroccan legislation on states of emergency is still vague, and said that it does not specify or place limits on the derogations that may be made from the provisions of the Covenant in emergencies and does not guarantee the implementation of article 4 of the Covenant. The committee had invited the State party to review the relevant provisions of its legislation in order to bring them fully into line with article 4 of the Covenant.

4. The Committee was concerned that, even though the death penalty has not been applied since 1994 and many of those sentenced to death have had their sentences commuted, the number of offences punishable by the death penalty has risen since the previous periodic report was considered (Covenant, art. 6). In accordance with article 6 of the Covenant, the committee urged Morocco to reduce to a minimum the number of offences punishable by the death penalty, with a view to abolishing capital punishment. The committee whished that the State party should also commute the sentences of all persons sentenced to death.

5. The Committee acknowledged the work done by the Consultative Council on Human Rights (CCDH) in the field of data collection and compensation in relation to disappeared persons, and said that it was concerned that those responsible for disappearances have still not been identified, tried and punished (Covenant, arts. 6 and 7). The Committee wished that the State party conduct the

necessary investigations to identify, try and punish those responsible for such crimes (Covenant, arts. 6 and 7).

6. The Committee was concerned that article 26 of the new law on the residence of aliens permits the immediate expulsion of an alien deemed to be a threat to State security, even if the alien may be subjected to torture or ill-treatment or sentenced to death in the receiving country. The committee urged the State party to set up a system that would allow any alien who claims that expulsion would put them at risk of being subjected to torture, ill-treatment or the death penalty to lodge an appeal that would have the effect of suspending the expulsion (Covenant, arts. 6, 7 and 10).

7. The Committee expressed concerns at the numerous allegations of torture and ill-treatment of detainees and at the fact that the officials who were guilty of such acts are generally liable to disciplinary action only, where any sanction exists. In this context, the Committee notes with concern that no independent inquiries are conducted in police stations and other places of detention in order to guarantee that no torture or ill-treatment takes place. The Committee said that the State party should ensure that complaints of torture and/or ill-treatment are examined promptly and independently. Also, It had said that conclusions of such examinations should be studied in depth by the relevant authorities so that those responsible can be not only disciplined but also punished under criminal law. All places of detention should be subject to independent inspection (Covenant, arts. 7 and 10).

8. The Committee considered the period of custody during which a suspect may be held without being brought before a judge—48 hours (renewable once) for ordinary crimes and 96 hours (renewable twice) for crimes related to terrorism—to be excessive. The State party was urged to review its legislation on custody with a view to bringing it into line with the provisions of article 9 and all the other provisions of the Covenant.

9. The Committee was concerned that the accused may have access to the services of a lawyer only from the time at which their custody is extended (that is, after 48 or 96 hours). It recalled that, in its previous decisions, it has held that the accused should receive effective assistance from a lawyer at every stage of the proceedings, especially in cases where the person may incur the death penalty. The Committee said that the State party should amend its legislation and practice to allow a person under arrest to have access to a lawyer from the beginning of their period in custody (Covenant, arts. 6, 7, 9, 10 and 14).

10. The Committee was concerned about the reports of poor conditions in prisons, particularly the shortage of medical care, the lack of rehabilitation programs and the lack of visiting areas (Covenant, arts. 7 and 10). The Committee urged the State party to improve prison conditions in line with article 10 of the Covenant and should institute alternative penalties.

11. The Committee was concerned that some representatives of non-governmental organizations had their passports confiscated and were thus prevented from attending a meeting of non-governmental organizations on the question of Western Sahara at the fifty-ninth session of the Commission on Human Rights in Geneva (Covenant, arts. 12 and 19). The Committee urged the State party to apply article 12 of the Covenant to all its nationals.

12. The Committee expressed concerns that the independence of the judiciary is not fully guaranteed, and urged that the State party should take the necessary steps to guarantee the independence and impartiality of the judiciary (Covenant, art. 14, para. 1).

13. The Committee was concerned that the Criminal Code permits any "serious attack using violence" to be classed as a terrorist act. It is also concerned about the numerous reports that the Anti-Terrorism Act adopted on 28 May 2003 is being applied retroactively. In order to rectify this situation of legal uncertainty, the Committee recommended that the State party should amend the

legislation in question by clearly defining its scope, and requests it
to ensure compliance with the provisions of article 15 and all the
other provisions of the Covenant.

14. The Committee was concerned about the de facto limitations on
the freedom of religion or belief, including the fact that it is
impossible, in practice, for a Muslim to change religion. It recalls
that article 18 of the Covenant protects all religions and all beliefs,
ancient and less ancient, major and minor, and includes the right
to adopt the religion or belief of one's choice. The committee
whished that the State party should take steps to ensure respect for
freedom of religion or belief and to ensure that its legislation and
practices are fully in conformity with article 18 of the Covenant.

15. The Committee noted that, according to the information sup-
plied by the State party, compulsory military service is a fallback
applicable only when not enough professional soldiers can be
recruited, while at the same time the State party does not recognize the right to conscientious objection. The committee urged
the State party to fully recognize the right to conscientious objection in times of compulsory military service and should establish
an alternative form of service, the terms of which should be nondiscriminatory (Covenant, arts. 18 and 26).

16. The Committee was concerned about the persistent reports that
journalists have been fined or harassed in the exercise of their profession. The Committee urged the State party to take the necessary measures to prevent any harassment of journalists and to
ensure that its legislation and practices give full effect to the
requirements of article 19 of the Covenant.

17. The Committee remained concerned that the process of issuing a
receipt for advance notice of meetings is often abused, which
amounts to a restriction on the right of assembly, as guaranteed by
article 21 of the Covenant. The Committee urged the State party
to eliminate the obstacles to the exercise of the right of assembly
(Covenant, art. 21).

18. The Committee had taken note of the various reports describing restrictions on the right to freedom of association. The Committee requested the State party to bring its practice into line with the provisions of article 22 of the Covenant.

19. While welcoming the progress made in the area of education, the Committee remained concerned about the continuing high number of illiterates, particularly among women. The Committee encouraged the State party to continue with the action undertaken to remedy this situation (Covenant, art. 26).

20. The Committee was concerned about the legal ban on marriages between women of the Muslim faith and men from other religions or with other beliefs (Covenant, arts. 3, 23 and 26). The Committee urged that the State party should comply with the provisions of articles 3, 23 and 26 of the Covenant by revising the legislation concerned.

21. The Committee was also concerned about the high level of domestic violence against women. The State party was urged to take suitable practical measures to combat this phenomenon (Covenant, arts. 3 and 7).

22. The Committee noted with concern that abortion is still a criminal offence under Moroccan law unless it is carried out to save the mother's life. The Committee had urged the State party to ensure that women are not forced to carry a pregnancy to full term where that would be incompatible with its obligations under the Covenant (arts. 6 and 7) and should relax the legislation relating to abortion.

23. The Committee regretted that the new Family Code, while placing limitations on the practice of polygamy, nevertheless does not ban it, despite the fact that it is detrimental to women's dignity (Covenant, arts. 3, 23 and 26). The Committee urged the State party should ban polygamy clearly and definitively (Covenant, arts. 3, 23 and 26).

24. The Committee noted that child labor was still widespread in
    Morocco, even though the new Labor Code prohibits work by
    children under the age of 15. The Committee urged the State
    Party is requested to take the measures envisaged to implement
    the provisions of the Labor Code in respect of minors (Covenant,
    art. 24).

25. The Committee noted that a child born of a Moroccan mother
    and a foreign father (or a father of unknown nationality) is treated
    differently from the children of a Moroccan father with regard to
    obtaining Moroccan nationality. The Committee urged the State
    party to comply with the provisions of article 24 of the Covenant
    and should ensure equal treatment for the children of a Moroccan
    mother and a Moroccan or foreign father (Covenant, arts. 24 and
    26).

26. While welcoming the adoption of the Family Code, the Commit-
    tee noted with concern that inequalities between women and men
    persist in the area of inheritance and divorce. The Committee
    urged the State party to review its legislation and ensure that any
    gender-based discrimination in the area of inheritance or divorce
    is eliminated (Covenant, art. 26).

The Human Rights Committee was more critical to Morocco than it
was in 1999. Terrorist attacks in Casablanca in May 16, 2001 were one of
the reasons that pushed the government to put security matters in front of
respect of human rights especially during investigation and detention.
This was against the King's will who declared in a speech after the events
that security and human rights should go hand in hand as the democratic
society requires.

2. Algeria: The failure of the State

In 2005, the Algerian President Abdelaziz Bouteflika declared that the
number of civil war casualties in his country at that time attended 200
thousands, including 60 journalists. Since 1992, the war started between

the official army and Salvation Islamic Army (AIS). When the right to life are threatened for all citizens of the country, all other rights are massively violated automatically. On 15 April 1998, four famous international human rights' NGOs (Amnesty International, Intenational Federation of Human Rights Leagues, Human Rights Watch and Repoter Without Borders) called on the UN Commission of Human Rights to face up its responsibility on Algeria. There were only seven working days left before the end of its session. They wrote: "Meanwile, in Algeria children continue to be hacked to death, women are abducted and raped, men are arrested at home and 'disappear' in the night (…) How many more dead will it take for the commission to stop turning a blind eye to the plight of the Algerian victims?" By the occasion, Pierre Sanné Secretary General of AI said that "inaction is tantamount of discriminating against victims of Algerian tragedy." While Joanna Weschler, representative at the UN of HRW added that "it is a crucial and necessary step to break the cycle of violence and impunity which reigns in Algeria today."

Algerian Governments were all the time attributing responsibility for massive killings to "terrorist groups" which means in the official political language Islamic armed groups. This was considered not convincing for AI that raised many questions about that:

> "How credible is this account?
> Consider, first, that most of the recent massacres have taken place in the most militarized region of the country—and often in the shadow of army barracks and security forces posts. The cries of the victims, the sounds of gunshots have been within earshot, and flames from burning houses have been visible in the distance. In some cases army units with armored vehicles were stationed nearby, yet no one intervened to stop the massacres. How is it possible that large bands of attackers could make their way to village, crossing main roads in highly controlled areas, carry out killings over several hours and then leave, unaccosted, on each occasion?
>
> Secondly, most massacres have taken place in areas where a large percentage of the population had voted for the now banned Islamic Salvation Front (FIS), before the cancellation of the electoral process and the imposition of the state of emergency in 1992. Victims of recent

massacres included FIS supporters, people who offered either active or passive support to armed "Islamist" groups, and individuals who had refused to join state-armed militias. Some of the massacres have allegedly been committed by groups acting on the instructions, or with the consent, of certain army and security forces units. Is it not possible that through the massacres, the government is physically seeking to 'eradicate' the Islamists it has vowed to destroy politically?

Thirdly, it may not be economic accident that the recent massacres have clustered around the Mitidja plateau near Algiers. This is the most fertile region of Algeria: its 500,000 acres were once the jewel of French Colonial agriculture. After independence, the land was nationalized and later farmers acquired the right to its permanent use. Recent efforts to privatize this land have sparked intense debate, and some fear that much of this rich land may finally wind up in the hands of powerful interest groups. Who stands to gain from massacres which have forced villagers and peasants to flee from the area?

These questions implicitly challenge the simplistic explanation—offered by Algerian officials to the international community—that the atrocities owe their sole origins to a conflict between a government that protect "democracy" and "terrorist groups" seeking to establish an "Islamic" regime."

In its second periodic report (CCPR/C/101/Add.1) presented on 18 May 1998, the Algerian government said that Islamic Salvation Front (FIS) did not hesitate "to 'justify' and 'legitimize' systematic attack on the fundamental human rights, especially the right to life and the the right to freedom of conscience." It adds that "Algerian people has been the constant target of terrorist attacks conducted by this party. The terrorist groups, which initially acted in the wake of the FIS, subsequently degenerated into a kind of mafia whose barbaric acts have no aim other than to burn, injure and kill, and to ruin the Algerian people, whom they regard as guilty for not having supported the reactionary model of society that they advocated" (pragraph 14 and 15).

After consideration of Algerian second periodic report (CCPR/C/101/ Add.1), the Committee on Civil and Political Rights concluded that:

1. There were widespread and indiscriminate attacks in Algeria against the civilian population, involving the loss of innumerable human lives, and a general climate of violence heighten the responsibilities of the state party to re-establish and maintain the conditions necessary for the enjoyment and protection of fundamental rights and freedoms;

2. Massacres of men, women, and children pushed the state to adopt effective measures: a) to prevent attacks and, if they nevertheless occur, to come promptly to the defense of the population; b) to ensure that proper investigations are conducted by an independent body to determine who the offenders are and to bring them to justice; and c) to conduct an independent enquiry into the conduct of security forces, from the lowest to the highest levels, and where appropriate, to subject them to penal and disciplinary sanctions;

3. The State (Algeria) did not give satisfactory responses to reports of arbitrary executions of individuals, some while in custody, others under suspicion of being associated in one way or another with terrorist groups;

4. "Legitimate defense groups" created by the regime, officially, to face armed groups, have no official recognition, competence, supervision and training. The Committee raised the legitimacy of the transfer of such power by the state to private groups;

5. There are allegations of systematic torture, and trial court judges accept confessions extracted under duress, even when there is medical evidence of torture;

6. The state failed to clarify cases of disappearances, and regarding their supposed large number, the state shall adopt measures; a) to establish a central register to record all reported cases of disappear-

ances and day-to-day action taken to retrace the disappeared; and
b) to assist the families concerned to retrace the disappeared.

7. There should be amendments to the Penal law to include a defini-
    tion of "terrorist" or "subversive" activities, and be brought into
    strict compliance with articles 6 and 9 of the Covenant.

In its annual report, AI said that the "level of violence and killings
diminished considerably in 1999, but remained nonetheless high." In July
1999, Civil Harmony Law was promulgated, by which members of armed
groups should surrender within six months to benefit from amnesty. This
law raised "concerns about impunity," said the same source. When Bouteflika became president, his priority was to bring peace, but massive killings
were renewed by the end of 2000.

The Committee on Civil and Political Rights expressed concerns about
massacres, but the states' counsels said that "terrorits" were responsible for
that. The same committee said that the Family Code "still contains important areas of inequality" between man and women. It had noted that
"under the family code, a woman's consent to her first marriage is generally mediated by a male guardian, and that this guardian can deny the
woman her choice of a husband to be the head of the family and for the
possibility of Polygamous marriage, and that it precludes a woman from
marrying a non-Muslim while the same restriction does not apply to a
man."

The same commission by the same occasion (In August 1998) stated
that the Arabic Language Decree came into force in July 1998 is exclusive,
and impede large sections of the population who use Berber [tamazight] in
the enjoyment of their cultural rights. Three years later, there was a resurrection in the country lead by people speaking berber. It took place mainly
in Tiziouzou. There were hundreds of casualties.

In July 2005, Algeria had not submitted to the Human Rights Committee the third periodic report that was due on June 1st, 2000. In 2005,
the Algerian League for the Defense of Human Rights (LADDH) reported
that many of its members were arrested in different times including Abder-
ahmane Khelil, a member of the Comité SOS-Disparus (SOS Committee

on Missing Persons) of the LADDH, who was first arrested in March and then in May 2002. Imprisoned in relation to investigations he had carried out regarding the arrest of several students from the University of Bouzaréah (Algiers) and charged with "encouraging non-armed gatherings", he was given a suspended 6-month prison sentence.

These cases, LADDH says, reveal how "obstacles are systematically placed in the way of all those who ask for light to be shed on the issue of missing persons and for justice." To an exemple, the LADDH stated that on Wednesday 3 July 2002, families of missing persons were not allowed to hold their weekly gathering in front of the headquarters of the Advisory Commission for the Defence and Promotion of Human Rights in Algiers. As a result the NGO said that demonstrators were violently dispersed and a great many women were wounded by truncheons.

The Algerian President Abdelaziz Bouteflika proposed a general amnesty for human rights abuses committed in the country since 1992. Many organizations include Amnesty International, Human Rights Watch, the International Center for Transitional Justice, the International Commission of Jurists and the International Federation for Human Rights, considered that the amnesty for the violations that took place during the brutal internal conflict in Algeria may permanently deprive victims or their families of their right to truth, justice and reparation. The President said that the amnesty law was a step towards "national reconciliation". He declared his intention to organize a referendum on the law.

3. Tunisia: The Most Protective the Most Abusive

When Zinalabidin Benali came to power in 1987, the Tunisians were hoping that he would end unique party system, and abuse of human rights. In 2001, unique party system ended, but human rights violations were more massive than they were. Freedom of expression suffers deeply; newspapers are totally owned by the state, or if independent, they are the president followers. Opposition is banned and its leaders persecuted. Human rights activists are either arrested or exiled. But at the same time written laws seem to be 'very' democratic. When presidential elections were organized in 1999, the government incited two candidates to be presented. One of them said that he was willing to vote for his rival the president Zinalabidin Benali (!!) Women's rights are more progressive in Tunisia than other North African Countries, although there are many remarks put by national human rights activists.

After the discussion of the Tunisian fourth periodic report (CCPR/C/ 84/Add.1) in October 1994, the Human Rights Committee had concluded that:

1.   There is a growing gap between law and practice with regard to guarantees and safeguards for the protection of human rights;

2.   There is no independent institution for promotion and defense of human rights. Consequently, the Committee notes that it is not clear whether the judiciary effectively monitor and enforce the implementation of existing human rights standards, including the investigation of abuses;

3.   There are reports of ill-treatment and torture of detainees, including death in custody under suspicious circumstances. Regulations aren't strictly adhered to with respect to the prompt registration of persons arrested, the immediate notification to family members, the limitation of pre-trial detention to 10-days maximum, the requirement of medical examinations whenever allegations of torture or other abuse and the carrying out of autopsies in all cases of death in custody;

4.   Government officials concerned with security matters who have been guilty of wrong-doing remain anonymous to the general public, which helps them to become immune from effective scrutiny;

5.   There is harassment of lawyers who have represented clients accused of having committed political offences;

6.   There are outdated legal provisions that concern status of married women and their equal rights in matters of child custody, the

transmission of nationality and parental consent for the marriage of minor children;

7. There are legal discrimination against non-Muslims with respect to eligibility for public office;

8. Freedom to criticize the government is not fully tolerated, and some fundamental freedoms are not fully enjoyed in practice. Many publications of foreign newspapers were banned, and sections of the Press Code dealing with defamation, insult and false information unduly limit the exercise of freedom of opinion and expression as provided for under article 19 of ICCPR. Offences carry severe penalties when criticism is directed against official bodies as well as the army or the administration, a situation which results in self-censorship by the media when reporting on public affairs.

9. Association Act may seriously undermine the enjoyment of the freedom of association, particularly with respect to the independence of human rights non-governmental organizations. Also, the Political Parties Act and the conditions imposed on the activities of political parties, do not appear to be in conformity with the right to association.

10. The ground for refusing a passport, under Passport Act, are not clearly specified by law, which leaves open the possibility of refusal on political or other unacceptable grounds; and

11. There is a well protected freedom to practice and manifest one's religion, but this right is not made available in respect of all beliefs.

In its fourth periodic report, Tunisia said that freedom of expression is guaranteed by article 8 of the constitution. The same report says that the right to hold opinion is guaranteed by law. About freedom of the press, the same official document says that it is forbidden to ban any publication by a simple decision of the Attorney General (Procureur de la Republique).

The abolition of a publication should be made after a decision of the primary court, while the minister of interior can ban any publication suspected of threatening the public order (l'ordre publique). This decision may be brought before a court. The report emphasized on laws more than practice. This is the reason why the Committee said that it was preoccupied by "the growing gap between law and Practice."

In its annual report (2001), AI said that there are "up to 1000 political prisoners" in Tunisia, and many political opponents "were subjected to harrassment and intimidation."

Freedom in the world report (1999–2000) published by Freedom House (FH) said that "Tunisians cannot change their government democratically," press freedom is "severely restricted," and permission is required for public gathering. FH adds that "general equality for women has advanced more in Tunisia than elsewhere in the Arab world. Inheritance is based on *Sharia* (Islamic law) and discriminates against women, although the government enacted legislation in 1998 to improve women's rights in matters of divorce and property ownership. Women are well represented in academics and in the professions. Twenty-one seats in the national legislature went to women following October 1999 elections." The same report remarked that Benali "offered a brief promise of an open political system. However his rule became increasingly autocratic and repressive."

Tunisia didn't present two due state's reports to the Human Rights Committee. In July 2005, it should have already submitted the fifth report on February 4th, 1998 and the sixth on the same date in 2003.

In its report "Tunisia: Crushing the Person Crushing a Movement" Human Rights Watch charged that the government's policy of isolation is driven not by legitimate penological concerns. Rather, this national policy seeks to punish and demoralize jailed leaders of the banned Nahdha (Renaissance) party, as part of government efforts to destroy the country's Islamist movement. The report stated that "not only does Tunisia's practice of long-term isolation violate international norms on the treatment of prisoners, it also violates Tunisian law" and urged Tunisian authorities to "end immediately the prolonged isolation of selected political prisoners."

By the same occasion, Human Rights Watch reaffirmed its call for the release of all prisoners in Tunisia who were convicted for the nonviolent exercise of their freedom of expression, association, and assembly. Also it had asked the government that all other prisoners who were convicted of politically motivated acts in proceedings that did not conform to international standards for a fair trial should either be freed or granted promptly new and fair trials.

Chocked by the ongoing abuses of human rights, seven political and independent personnalities undertook in october 2005 an unlimited hunger strike claiming reforms and democratic change. Before that, they issued a call to the public opinion stating that Tunisia "has been living for years a deteroration of its political, social and cultural situation."(11)

4. Libya: The Desert of Individual Rights

Libya submits its reports to the treaty bodies of the United Nations in the due time. It was an exception in North African Countries until 2002 when Libya failed to submit its fourth report to the Human Rights Committee due on October 10th, 2002. In 2005, it had submitted 30 reports to different treaty bodies of the United Nations. Most of them were submitted before the prescribed date. Libya considers that "the Green Book" theory is based on human rights if not it is human rights in itself. For Kadhafi "Aljamahiria" regime is better than democracy, but for human rights analysts it is an absolute dictatorship.

There are no democratic elections based on pluralism. There is another kind of 'election' by which people choose their representatives in the People's General Congress (a kind of parliament). This is not looked at as respectful of international standards of human rights. In fact, Libyan citizens cannot change their government, and free media do not exist at all. FH reported that "independent political parties and civic associations are illegal; only associations affiliated with the regime are tolerated. Political activity considered treasonous acts are punishable by death." The same report adds that "women's access to education and employment have improved under the current regime." Kaddafi abolished polygamy against the traditions of his country. Recently women's revolutionary committee proposed to come back on this decision, but it was severly refused by Kaddafi himself who had stated by the same occasion that "polygamy is a kind of servitude and has nothing to do with religion." Also, Kaddafi presents himself as a religious leader who leads prayers.

The committee on Civil and Political rights considered Libyan Arab Jamahiria third periodic report (CCPR/C/102/add.1) and adopted the following remarks:

1. There are allegations of extra judicial, arbitrary or summary executions perpetrated by state agents as well as of a high incidence of arbitrary arrest and detention, including long detention without trial. The Committee urged the state to include in the fourth report names and statistics of disappeared persons, cases of extra judicial, arbitrary or summary executions about persons kept under detention without charge, in situation of indefinite detention without trial or following acquittal by courts;

2. Death penalty is imposed for offences which cannot be characterized as the most serious, including political and economic offences;

3. There are allegations of systematic use of torture and cruel, inhuman or degrading treatment or punishment;

4. Flogging is recognized in the Libyan Arab Jamahirya as a penalty for criminal offences. The Committee urges that this practice should cease immediately and all laws and regulations providing for its imposition should be repealed without delay;

5. The law enacted in 1997 known as the "Charter of Honor" which authorizes collevtive punishment for those found guilty of collective crimes (including "obstructing the people's authority, damaging public and private institutions), permits torture, cruel, inhuman, and degrading punishment;

6. There is excessive duration of remand in custody and indue prolongation of re-trial detention;

7. There are doubts about the independence of the judiciary and the liberty of advocates to exercise their profession freely, without being in the employment of the state;

8. There are numerous restrictions, in law and in practice, on the right to freedom of expression, and in particular on the right to express opposition to or criticism of the government;

9. there is discrimination in law and practice against children born out of wedlock;

10. Minority rights are violated, and more than that the state declares that there are no ethnic, cultural minorities in the country.

The Committee on Civil and Political Rights urged Libya to rectify the situation, and observed that although the Libyan government became a party to the Optional Protocol in 1989, only two communication and three contact letters have been addressed to the committee. The Committee concluded that this "may suggest that the people living in the state party are not aware of their right to use such mechanisms."

The state's report emphasized that the "political system in the Socialist People's Jamahiria is based on direct popular democracy in which the masses play their political, economic and social role and take decisions concerning various aspects of public and private life."

In its annual report of 2001, AI declared that in Libya there are "no independent non-governmental organizations, human rights groups or independent bar association." The same international NGO said that "five prisoners of conscience, who were arrested in 1973 and convicted of membership of the prohibited Islamic Liberation Party, continued to serve life sentences in Abu Salim Prison in Tripoli." It adds that "several people, including possible prisoners of conscience (…) are in detention." Some of them belong to Jama'a al-Islamia al-Libiya (the Libyan Islamic Group). AI reveals the names of Rashid 'Abdal-Hamid al-'Urfia, and Al-Sayyid Mohammed Shabou. The first, a law graduate was arrested with 20 others in 1982 on suspicion of founding an Islamic opposition group. The second, also a Libyan with connection to Islamic opposition, he was detained by the Libyan authorities after he and his family were forcibly returned to Libya. He continued to be held without charges or trial, reportedly in connection with his Islamist opposition activities.

'Disappearance' of Mansor Kikhya, an opposition Libyan leader and human rights activists, in Cairo in 1993, was put by many human rights activists on Libyan government's back. Kaddafi denied having any relation with Kikhya disappearance, and received his wife Baha al-Emri in Libya, and the reception was broadcasted through television. Kikhya fate is still unknown by courts. In February 1999, an Egyptian court of appeals ordered the state to pay compensation for Kikhya's wife because the state failed to protect a foreigner on its territory, but the court of cassation suspended the ruling.

Human Rights Watch reported that over the past three decades, Libya's human rights record has been appalling. The international NGO said that abuse in Libya include the abduction, forced disappearance or assassination of political opponents; torture and mistreatment of detainees; and long-term detention without charge or trial or after grossly unfair trials. HRW emphasised that hundreds of people remain arbitrarily detained, some for over a decade, and there are serious concerns about treatment in detention and the fairness of procedures in several on-going high profile trials before the Peoples' Courts. Libya hasd been a closed country for United Nations and non-governmental human rights investigators till 2005 when it had authorized HRW to its first-ever visit to the country.

After the visit the NGO stated that serious problems remained, including the use of violence against detainees, restrictions on freedom of expression and association, and the incarceration of political prisoners.

During Human Rights Watch's three-week mission to Libya, the authorities provided access to a wide range of high-level officials, as well as police stations, an immigration detention center, five prisons and more than two dozen prisoners, who were interviewed in private. Government guides, however, escorted Human Rights Watch researchers and controlled unauthorized contact with individuals. "The Libyan government's invitation reflected a welcome degree of transparency," said Sarah Leah Whitson, Middle East and North Africa director at Human Rights Watch.

5. Egypt: Religious Intolerance

Egyptian judiciary is the strongest in the Arab world. Due to judges and lawyers, courts took courageous decision such as that related to Kikhya case in 1999. But another court ordered divorce of a secular intellectual from his wife against the couple's will, because it was thought that secularism is a sort of atheism, and a Muslim woman should be married only to a believer in God and the prophet Mohammed. Although the intellectual, Nasser Hamid Abou-Zid, declared that he has never been an atheist and he is a Muslim, he has not been heard. To keep on living with his wife in wedlock, he was self exiled in Europe. A Cairo court ordered the state to pay $9.000 to each of two Muslim activists detained in 1950s, for physical and mental torture suffered in prison. In August 1999, a higher administrative court in August annulled a presidential order to send 77 suspected Islamic militants to a military trial, calling the case a civil one, reported FH. But successive laws are trying to limit independence of the judiciary. Law 47/1972 allowed the justice minister to interfere with judicial rulings at will. Under law 25/1996, the president may refer civilian cases to military courts.

Egyptian Organization of Human Rights (EOHR) is a very active NGO that criticizes severely the government about the abuses it commits. In 2000, it declared that "five people died in police stations between February and July 1999 as a result of torture by police. Another was reportedly tortured to death in October. Police are rarely held accountable for such cases. In May, charges were dropped against four police officers implicated in the arrest and torture of nearly 1.200 Christians in the fall of 1998."

In 2001, Egypt had two due reports to the Committee on Civil and Political rights, the third on 31 December 1994, and the fourth on 13 April 1998. The initial report was presented one year late, and the second four years behind schedule. While considering the late report (CCPR/C/51/Add.71), the Committee made the following conclusions:

1. Increasing number of terrorist acts created a dramatic situation in the country. However, the Committee considers that definition of terrorism contained in law number 97 adopted in 1992, is so broad that it encompasses a wide range of acts of differing gravity, and it enlarges the number of offences which are punishable with the death penalty [according to article 6 of the ICCPR only the most serious crimes may lead to the death penalty].

2. Emergency Act entitled the President of the Republic to refer cases to the state security courts, to ratify judgments and to pardon. This makes the President's role part of the executive and part of the judiciary system.

3. The duration and conditions of police custody and administrative detention are likely to expose accused persons to torture and ill-treatment by the police and security forces. The Committee urged Egypt to investigate and apply penalties to perpetrations, and compensate victims of torture.

4. There is a multitude of special courts in Egypt. The Committee noticed that legal consistency in the judicial procedure and procedural guarantees it is important that special courts exist as an exceptional measure, if at all.

5. There are many legal restrictive provisions of freedom of thought, conscience, religion, assembly and association.

6. Egypt denies the existence in the country of religious or other minorities, as there are laws with provisions containing penalties of imprisonment with compulsory labor for political offences. Also, the Committee observes that, in many areas, law discriminates against women and restricts them in the equal enjoyment of rights and freedoms.

In its annual report 2001, Human Rights Watch said that the government "intensified its efforts to exercise control over civil society institutions, harassing and restricting the activities of political parties, human rights and other non governmental organizations (NGOs), professional associations and the press." The report adds that "in May 20, the political parties committee of the Majlis al-shura (parliament) froze the activities of the islamist opposition. Labor Party and banned its publications, ostensibly because of a leadership dispute within the party. This action, widely perceived as part of an attempt to silence government critics ahead of the elections, followed violent street demonstrations, followed violent street demonstrations in early May over the publication of a novel alleged to be offensive to Islam. The Labor Party's bi-weekly newspaper, al-Sha'ab, had denounced the novel. Despite several court ruling in favor of the party, the ban on its publications remained in force as of October 2000."

In Egypt, a citizen may be deprived from his civil and political rights if his views are not accepted by someone else who may go to court and sue a person for having a "blasphemous" view, or practicing something considered "not harmonious" with Islam as it was for Nasser Hamid Abou-Zid and Naouale Al-Saadaoui cases. Al-Saadaoui's writings were blaimed of being against Islam. In November 1999, when the ministry of culture authorized the re-printing of a novel titled *"A banquet of Seaweed"* by Syrian author Haidar Haidar, there were demonstrations in streets and universities demanding the government to ban the novel. The government ended by withdrawing the book from the market.

It was also reported that the right to freedom of conscience and religion had been violated. AI, HRW, and FIDH published reports about al-Kusheh case. During a financial dispute between a Muslim and a Coptic Christian, a Coptic made offensive remarks which were considered against Islam. This had led to three days of rioting, and 23 people were dead. Many citizens were arrested and tried on murder, attempted murder, incitement to violence, robbery, and other charges. The European Parliament considered this conflict between Copts and Muslims, and called Egypt to "raise awareness about religious tolerance and respect for human rights and minority freedoms by launching a campaign on sectarian hatred and violence."

An Egyptian tribunal condemned the American-Egyptian intellectual Sa^ad Ed-din Ibrahim for many years of prison for receiving foreign funds to support his NGO. This condemnation was a result of a long scrutiny of NGOs' activities. Before the government was trying to apply a controversial Law on Civil Associations and Institutions (Law 153 of 1999) opposed by the whole national and international civil society, because they considered that it permits interference in NGOs' internal affairs. The Supreme Constitutional Court overturned this law as it was not presented to parliament, which was welcomed by human rights activists.

In its concluding observations to Egypt's third report (CCPR/CO/76/EGY—Egypt. 28/11/2002), the Human Rights Committee regretted the seven-year delay in submission of the third periodic report (due in 2002) and pointed out that "conflating two reports into one should be avoided in the future."

After it had welcomed some initiatives taken by the State party as regards human rights, in particular the creation of human rights divisions within the ministries of justice and foreign affairs and the introduction of human rights training and awareness programs at schools and universities for law-enforcers and society at large, the Committee expressed its concerns as follows:

1. The Committee said that it was disturbed by the fact that the state of emergency proclaimed by Egypt in 1981 is still in effect, meaning that the State party has been in a semi-permanent state of emergency ever since. The Committee urged the State party to consider reviewing the need to maintain the state of emergency.

2. The Committee noted that women are underrepresented in most areas of the public sector (for instance, the magistrate) and in the private sector (articles 3 and 26 of the Covenant). The Committee encouraged Egypt to step up its efforts to secure greater participation by women at all levels of society and the State, including

decision-making positions, inter alia by ensuring that women in rural areas learn to read and write.

3.   The Committee noted with concern that women seeking divorce through unilateral repudiation by virtue of Act No. 1 of 2000 must forego their rights to financial support and, in particular, to their dowries (articles 3 and 26 of the Covenant). The Committee proposed to the State party to review its legislation so as to eliminate financial discrimination against women.

4.   The Committee noted the discriminatory nature of some provisions in the Penal Code, which do not treat men and women equally in matters of adultery (articles 3 and 26 of the Covenant).The Committee said that the State party had to review its discriminatory penal provisions in order to conform to articles 3 and 26 of the Covenant.

5.   The Committee drew attention to the discrimination affecting women as regards transmission of nationality to their children when their spouses are not Egyptian and as regards the rules governing inheritance (articles 3 and 26 of the Covenant). It had encouraged the State party to bring its current inquiries to a conclusion and do away with all discrimination between men and women in its domestic legislation.

6.   While taking note of the action and awareness campaigns against female genital mutilation, the Committee noted that this practice still continues (article 7 of the Covenant). The Committee urged the State party to eradicate the practice of female genital mutilation.

7.   The Committee noted with concern the very large number of offences which, under Egyptian law, are punishable by the death penalty, and the incompatibility of certain of those offences with article 6, paragraph 2, of the Covenant. The State party should review the question of the death penalty in light of the provisions of article 6 of the Covenant. The State party was also asked to pro-

vide the Committee with detailed information on the number of offences which carry the death penalty, the number of people sentenced to death, the number of those executed, and the number of sentences commuted since 2000. The Committee called on the State party to bring its legislation and practice into line with the Covenant. The Committee recommends that Egypt take measures to abolish the death penalty.

8. While noting the creation of institutional machinery and the introduction of measures to punish any violations of human rights by employees of the State, the Committee noted with concern the persistence of torture and cruel, inhuman or degrading treatment at the hands of law-enforcement personnel, in particular the security services, whose recourse to such practices appears to display a systematic pattern. It is equally concerned at the general lack of investigations into such practices, punishment of those responsible, and reparation for the victims. It is also concerned at the absence of any independent body to investigate such complaints (articles 6 and 7 of the Covenant). The Committee concluded that the State party should ensure that all violations of articles 6 and 7 of the Covenant are investigated and, depending on the results of investigations, should take action against those held responsible and makes reparation to the victims. It should also set up an independent body to investigate such complaints. The State party is invited to provide detailed statistics in its next report on the number of complaints lodged against State employees, the nature of the offences alleged, the State services implicated, the number and nature of the enquiries launched, the action taken, and the reparations made to the victims.

9. The Committee regretted the lack of clarity about the law and practice in matters of detention in custody: the duration of such detention, and access to a lawyer during such detention. It pointed out that it has been given no information on the total duration of pre-trial detention or the offences involved. It is con-

cerned at the lack of clarity concerning the safeguards laid down in article 9, paragraph 3, of the Covenant. The Committee also notes the persistent occurrence of cases of arbitrary detention. The Committee requested the State party to elaborate on the compatibility of its legislation and practice in matters of detention in custody and pre-trial detention with article 9 of the Covenant.

10. While noting the explanations given by the delegation of the State party about the periodic and spontaneous inspections of prison establishments by the authorities, the Committee notes that detention conditions inconsistent with article 10 of the Covenant persist. It also regrets the impediments to visits by United Nations-instituted treaty and non-treaty human rights mechanisms and non-governmental human rights organizations. The Committee invited the State party to provide the Committee in its next report with statistics on the number of people set free as a result of inspections. It is also encouraged to permit intergovernmental and non-governmental visits and ensure that, in actual practice, article 10 of the Covenant is strictly respected.

11. While understanding the security requirements associated with efforts to combat terrorism, the Committee voices concern at their effects on the human rights situation in Egypt, particularly in relation to articles 6, 7, 9 and 14 of the Covenant. In relation to this issue the Committee made the following remarks:

   a. The Committee considered that the effect of the very broad and general definition of terrorism given in Act No. 97 of 1992 is to increase the number of offences attracting the death penalty in a way that runs counter to the sense of article 6, paragraph 2, of the Covenant.

   b. The Committee noted with alarm that military courts and State security courts have jurisdiction to try civilians accused of terrorism although there are no guarantees of those courts' independence and their decisions are not subject to appeal before a higher court (article 14 of the Covenant).

c. The Committee noted furthermore that Egyptian nationals
suspected or convicted of terrorism abroad and expelled to
Egypt have not benefited in detention from the safeguards
required to ensure that they are not ill-treated, having notably
been held incommunicado for periods of over one month
(articles 7 and 9 of the Covenant).

The Committee urged the State party to ensure that steps taken in
the campaign against terrorism are fully in accordance with the
Covenant. It should ensure that legitimate action against terrorism does not become a source of violations of the Covenant.

12. The Committee expressed concerns about infringements of the
right to freedom of religion or belief and made the following
remarks:

a. The Committee deplored the ban on worship imposed on the
Bahai community.

b. The Committee was also concerned at the pressures applied
to the judiciary by extremists claiming to represent Islam,
who have even succeeded, in some cases, in imposing on
courts their own interpretation of the religion (articles 14, 18
and 19 of the Covenant).

The Committee urged the State party to review its legislation and
practice to make it consistent with article 18 of the Covenant as
regards the rights of the Bahai community and reinforce its legislation, in particular Act No. 3 of 1996, to make it consistent with
articles 14, 18 and 19 of the Covenant.

13. The Committee was deeply concerned at the State party's failure
to take action following the publication of some very violent articles against the Jews in the Egyptian press, which in fact constitute
advocacy of racial and religious hatred and incitement to discrimination, hostility and violence. The Committee urged the State
party to take whatever action is necessary to punish such acts by
ensuring respect for article 20, paragraph 2, of the Covenant.

14. The Committee noted the criminalization of some behaviors such as those characterized as "debauchery" (articles 17 and 26 of the Covenant). The Committee urged the State party to ensure that articles 17 and 26 of the Covenant are strictly upheld, and should refrain from penalizing private sexual relations between consenting adults.

15. While noting the efforts the State party has made to ensure that people are educated about human rights and tolerance, the Committee observed that results in this area are still inadequate. The Committee invited the State party to strengthen human rights education and use education to forestall all displays of intolerance and discrimination based on religion or belief.

16. The Committee was concerned at the restrictions placed by Egyptian legislation and practice on the foundation of non-governmental organizations and the activities of such organizations such as efforts to secure foreign funding, which require prior approval from the authorities on pain of criminal penalties (article 22 of the Covenant).The Committee encouraged the State party to review its legislation and practice in order to enable non-governmental organizations to discharge their functions without impediments which are inconsistent with the provisions of article 22 of the Covenant, such as prior authorization, funding controls and administrative dissolution.

17. The Committee noted the de jure and de facto impediments to the establishment and functioning of political parties, primarily created by the committee set up under the Political Parties Act No. 40 of 1977, without full guarantees of independence (articles 22 and 25 of the Covenant). The Committee urged the State party to permit the democratic expression of political pluralism and thus abide by its obligations under the Covenant, taking into account the Committee's General Comment No. 25. It is also requested to provide in its next report a list of the offences for

which a court may strip individuals of their civil and political rights.

The Human Rights Committee adopted new guidelines that had been effective for reports since December 31st, 1999. North African countries' reports after and before the date (see above) show the big differences (HRI/GEN/2/Rev.2).

The Committee urged States parties to take the concluding observations as a starting point while reporting about the enjoyment of the Covenant rights. The proposed structure "forced" States parties to be direct. By the same occasion, it stated that "periodic reports should be structured so as to follow the articles of the Covenant." The guidelines suggested that "if there is nothing new to report under any article, it should be stated."

CONCLUSION: THE MAIN THREATS

Human rights are essential to both human lives and governance. At the beginning of the new millenium, human rights in NAC got a new dimension. Governments can not say openly that they are against human rights as they used to do in recent decades. NGOs are getting stronger more and more. Their cooperation with international NGOs helps them to acquire strength, experience, and professionalism. The main threat to human rights in NAC is represented by obscurantist movements, illiteracy, and social suffering. Education on human rights is the key to promote people's understanding of human rights and anchoring of their value in citizen's daily behavior. Also, governments went on to be a major handicap to the implementation of human rights. The elite's interests, the economic interests, and active actors during the darkest periods of their country's history, are all against any evolution in favor of human rights.

Unfortunately, the political elite is not very sensitive to human rights. Only some ex-communist movements turned to human rights supporters after they had been using human rights just to defend themselves against oppression. For this reason, We find that of human rights activists were victims. The so-called "liberals" do not care about human rights. Most of them are deeply linked either to states or to obscurantist spheres.

For the state's apparatus, the guarantees for the protection of human rights are: (a) an accountable system; and (b) a fair democracy where decision makers should be elected through free and fair elections. But this is conditioned by the existence of active and strong political parties.

---

(1) Iain Mclean. Oxford Concise Dictionary of Politics. Ed. Oxford University Press. Oxford, New York. P.464.

(2) Roger Scruton. A Dictionary of Political Thought. Second Edition. Ed. Macmillan. P. 522-523.

(3) Ibid.

(4) e.g. Bouteflika in response to Amnesty International after asking about the possibility to investigate inside Algeria for the reasons of massive killings in the civil war since 1992.

(5) The Universal Declaration of Human Rights. ART.2.

(6) Optional Protocol to the ICCPR. ART.5.

(7) Ibid. ART. 5(2).

(8) Human Rights Watch. Annual Report 2000. (The Introduction).

(9) Stephanie Lagoutte and Aygust Thor Arnason. Article 16 [of the UDHR]. In The Universal Declaration Of Human Rights—A Common Achievment. Edited by Gudmander Alfredson and Asbjorn Eid. Martinus Nijhoff Publishers, The Hague/Boston/London. 1999. p.326.

(10) Ibid. p.327.

(11) http://cyber.law.harvard.edu/globalvoices/2005/10/18/tunisia-hunger-strike-and-censorship/

PART III

VII. Political Parties Tools For Good Governance

INTRODUCTION

Six years after its independence in 1956, pluralism was proclaimed in Moroccan's constitution. But the one-party state did not fade till recent years in Egypt, Tunisia, and Algeria. In Libya there is still the regime of Kaddafi based on "non-political party regime," but in reality there is Aljamahiria party, which is based on the doctrine of "The Green Book". In Libya the state and the party are one thing, and citizens are supposed to be "Aljamahiria" members. Before, Nasser, Bourguiba, and Boumedien did the same as Kaddafi. They built unique parties for pluralistic societies, plural in their thoughts, political tendencies, habits, and religious believes sometimes. This way of governing forced opposition parties to live underground. But from time to time, bloody insurrections brought new lives to them. Military oppression always puts down any opposition that expresses itself. But opposition movements rise from their ashes, although there were thousands of political detainees, and hundreds of asylum seekers. The opposition used to reorganize itself and struggle against oppression, and for the right to freedom of speech and the right to association.

The political parties are important tools for good governance. This may be an obvious idea for any advanced country. But for underdeveloped countries, this is a matter that raises discussions, because governance is sometimes practiced without the political parties. When the government isn't clearly drawn from the majority after fair and free elections, the presence of political parties in the political scene is useless. Good governance may be assured in a political system only if political parties are heard, and their position in society is strong. Their members should be credible by their professionalism and common sense. Also, their creativeness, internal democracy, and full independence towards administrative authorities, should be unfailingly.

In North African Countries (NAC), a political majority within parliament, except for Libya, supports governments because there are no political parties and no parliament. In Algeria, Tunisia, and Egypt governments are drawn from the majority, but elections are unfair and opposition is outlawed. In Morocco, after many years of oppression, the opposition could influence the political scene, and in 1998 it formed the cabinet. Though all political parties praised the elections of the House of Representatives members that took place in September 2002, Local elections of September 2003, were criticized by the opposition and the majority itself as being unfair, but it is "more developed than it was in the 1980s when deaths were able to vote and throw down the socialists" But every country has its specific features.

In Morocco, there are eight major political parties, and many small political groups. Six of the major ones had governed during different periods. But their governance was in partnership with the king, as the king in Morocco reigns and rules. At the same time no one of them had declared that he had one day disagreed with the king about any decision. The socialist used to do so when they were in the opposition, but once they accepted to participate in the cabinet, they had ceased to do so. The extremist Islamist party called "Justice and charity" went on criticizing the king openly. But the moderate Islamist party "Justice and development" says that their colleague's positions are more extremists, and urges them to criticize the government alone. The King Mohammed VI has neither opposed nor responded those who criticized him. Also, the government went on being criticized bitterly. Either in parliament or in the press no one spares different ministers. Most of the time, ministers choose to respond to critics published in the press, but in parliament they are obliged to.

Recently, citizens started to avoid belonging to political parties, because they lost credibility. Most of the people consider that all political leaders are opportunists. This is a wrong common idea, enforced by parties' passiveness and lack of renewing generations. In their political bureau, there are in no leader fewer than 40. All over the world the youth prefers to go to a concert than to attend a political ceremony and hear successive political speakers. But for NAC there is a gap between youth and political parties. Most of them choose extremist groups. Conscious of this situation talked about by the king himself in the throne speech, political parties started in 2001 to organize their general assemblies. Through the periodicity of their assemblies are provided by their internal laws, it has never been respected. The Ministry of interior prepared in 2004 a draft law saying that political parties that doesn't respect delays provided by their internal laws that should be based on democratic principles would be deprived of state's financial subsidies.

A. MOROCCO: ROOTED PLURALISM AND LACK OF PROFESSIONALISM

Political parties in Morocco, all tendencies included, would have been a determinant factor to good governance if they were more credible than what they are. Some parties were weakened by oppression, and some others became incredible because of exaggerating the use of their parties for self-interests. But with the 2005's political parties' law that enforces internal democracy, accountability and guarantees public funding, political parties may be more active in the future, which may help them to take important decisions, and to experience professionalism.

Political parties in Morocco are of different tendencies. Some of them were harshly treated by the regime. Many movements were banned. They include Marxists, Islamists, and extremist nationalists who believe in the supremacy of the Moroccan nation, which they consider that it is made of Berbers. Nearly in each decade there was a resurrection. In 1958, two years after the independence, the north went into a wide armed opposition wave. This opposition led by local leaders did not want the national party called "Istiklal" (the independence) to govern. On March 23rd, 1965, people in many cities went to streets to claim good living standards, especially in Casablanca and Rabat (Middle West). Demonstrators considered that the independence brought nothing to them. In the early 1970s coup led consequently by Col. Medbouh, and Gen. Oufkir, and student's eruption to the streets calling for democracy, were the most important events. In 1981, 1984, and 1990 many angry demonstrations expressed their disagreement about the economic policies taken by governments of those days. Six resurrections, six constitutions and seven parliaments made Moroccan political life the most active in North Africa. This is the reason why in Morocco it was possible that the opposition came to power in 1998 by the help of a large coalition led by the National Gathering of Independents (RNI), the party which had the majority in both houses of parliament and that was considered as "the King's party."

King Hassan II urged two of his Prime Ministers to form their political parties. The first was Ahmed Osman who founded the above-mentioned RNI, and the second was Maâti Bouabid who built the Constitutional Union (UC). The first has easily turned to a real political party, while the second stood manipulated by the Ministry of Interior. There was a long quarrel between the RNI and Basri who was minister of the interior for more than 20 years continuously. This quarrel was about the independence of the RNI towards the state, and its members' right to make coalition with whom they want. This ended by RNI's coalition with the socialist opposition.

All Moroccan political parties agree upon monarchy. There are discussions if the King should rule or just reign, but till 2005 there were only two citizens who called for a republican regime. Those who used to claim such position in the 1970s were the Marxists and the Islamist populists. Actually they ended by recognizing the monarchy. The Islamists founded their political party "Justice and Development" and the Marxists have their owns. The first exception was with Abdelah Zaâzaâ who is issued from the Marxist-Leninist tendency and the second is Nadia Yassin one of the leaders of "Justice and Charity Movement." Both called for the republic. These positions raised stormy opposition inside the Moroccan elites who declared themselves ready to fight for the monarchy.

B. ALGERIA: THE UNPREPARED PLURALISM

In Algeria, the resurrection of 1988 was the last step towards breaking the unique party regime. In 1987 a new constitution tolerated pluralism. Many new political parties were founded. The Islamic movement of Abassi Madani the Islamic Salvation Front (FIS) started to influence the public opinion. It called for democratic presidential and parliamentary elections, and they proposed to change the law by *Sharia*. The party of Hussein Aït Ahmed came to the surface after many years of work underground. It is based on Berbers, people speaking a local language called *Tamazight*. This party wanted *Tamazight* to be the official language of the country, and the full democratization of the country. One smaller party led by Said Saâdi named the Gathering for culture and Democracy (RCD) was founded on the same basis. Ahmed Benbela the first president of Algeria also founded his party after he came back from exile in 1990. Many other parties came to life.

When the first pluralistic elections took place, Algeria was put in an oven. The first of the two rounds electoral system gave the majority to the FIS. The military leaders were afraid of the Islamists to take the parliament. They forced the President of the Republic at that time Chadli Benjdid to resign, and stopped the electoral process as a whole, and put most of the successful members of parliament under police control. The Islamists considered the regime unlawful and declared the civil war.

After many thousands of casualties, the president Lyamin Zeroual founded his own party the Democratic National Rally (RND) and called for parliamentary elections in 1997. Although the Socialist Forces Front (FFS) boycotted them, a new parliament was in place. Pretending illness, Zeroual called for new presidential elections in 1999. These elections brought Abdelaziz Bouteflika to presidency. The army supported him and the ex-unique party the National Liberation Front (FLN), which made the political elite, asks again the question of the credibility of political parties in the Algerian political system.

In 2005, there were over than 45 legal parties. Surely most of them were ridiculous, but important ones are less than eight. The army manipulates

RND and FLN. The FFS and the Workers Party represented the secular opposition. The Rally for Culture and Democracy (RCD), a harsh opposition to Islamists, participated in Bouteflika's cabinet after his election president of the republic. The Movement of a Peaceful Society (MSP) mainly forms the Islamist opposition.

The political intervention of the army, and the civil war had weakened all political activists. Abortion of democracy in 1992, gave way to loss of confidence. Also, this is why in April 1999, at the eve of the day of presidential elections all candidates of the political parties resigned and accused Bouteflika (independent) of having already planned to his success with the army against the Algerians will.

Real opposition is either outlawed or harshly treated. Two parties mainly represent it: The FIS and the FFS. The later led Tizi Ouzou resurrection after some of the law enforcement officials killed a young man in this city. The failure to solve the problem peacefully resulted in riot and killings. Opposition said that if the government had accepted its claims and opened the way to negotiations, there would not have been that high number or casualties, and heavy costs of loss.

Political parties and the government, which is influenced by the army, should restore trust. In 1995, some Algerian political parties drafted a peace plan after a national conference in Rome. This group was called "National Charter Group." The military, pretending that this plan was held out of the country, did not recognize it. Experts of conflicts advance actually the principle of "talks about talks" or pre-negotiation (p66). Its importance "can not be overstated. Bad process will almost definitely lead to failure: what may seem dry and technical procedural questions need to be resolved prior to talks (...) pre-negotiation can shade into negotiation if it goes extremely well." (p67)

On March 6th, 1997 the organic law that governs political parties was amended. Article three of this law stipulates that political parties, in their activities, must refrain from using Islamic, Arab and Amazigh identities for partisan purpose.

The political system in Algeria protects FLN hegemony.. This parti had dominated the political scene since the independence. In October 2003, when its Secretary General Ali Benflis was candidate to presidency, some of its prominent members supported Abdelazizi Bouteflika. The pro-Bouteflika fraction succeeded at the end to take the leadership and ousted Benflis.

C. TUNISIA: THE OPPRESSED OPPOSITION

In Tunisia, there are three main political parties: the official ruling party the Constitutional Democratic Rally Party (RCD) of the president of the republic Zinalabidin Benali, the Islamist outlawed party Annahda (the resurrection), and the socialist party the Movement of Democratic Socialists (MDS). The small groups are about five including the Communist Party, which has been a legal party since 1983. The official ruling party RCD gives no opportunity to the opposition to express itself. The President appoints members of RCD Political Bureau as he appoints members of his cabinet and high state officials. RCD members had not the right to change their national leadership. On 25 July 2001, the human rights activists and opposition leader Muncif Marzouki founded a new political party. It is called the "Congress for the Republic". Marzouki declared that his main aim is to enforce democracy and force the president Benali to respect the constitution by not being candidate to presidential elections for the fourth time in 2004. But the constitution was amended and Benali re-elected. The RCD launched an underground campaign to amend article 39 of the constitution, which was providing that the same president should not be elected for more than three terms of office.

Till 2005, the political parties do not participate in government and they are victims of "bad governance" based on persecution of democrats and institutions are not drawn from fair elections. The RCD is in power since 1963 when the Communist Party was banned (Jan.8th), and as a matter of fact, the New Constitutional Party founded the one-party regime, before changing its name to the Socialist Constitutional Party in 1964. The ex-president Habib Bourguiba who «resigned» for health reasons in 1987 founded it. There is an official opposition represented by two small parties, but there is the real opposition represented by MDS and

Annahda. These parties tried vainly to participate in recent presidential elections on October 24th, 1999. MDS was prevented from participation, and as Annahda was banned since 1986, it was impossible for any of its members to be candidates.

D. LIBYA: THE PARTY IS THE STATE

In Libya there are no political parties. All Citizens are considered members of Aljamahiria (the state). This state works as a political party in its design. The outlawed opposition is represented by Aljamaâ al-Islamia. There are several groups living outside Libya, especially in Europe and the USA, who claim to be an opposition to Kadhafi, but they have no influence upon citizens. Some activists of Aljamaâ al-Islamia are spending prison sentences in jails, and some of them led the resurrection of July 1995. What may be considered a grain of an opposition at the beginning of 21st century, may flourish during the coming up years. The regime itself may try a policy based on gradual openness, but this is conditioned by re-organizing the whole system to be based on democracy, and this depends on the leader of the revolution himself. All the books and essays he wrote were devoted to his revolutionary ideas. So, how can he change his ideas by his will? The evolution in Egypt was made after Nasser's death. Will Libyans wait till Kaddafi's death to live in a democratic country?

E. EGYPT: MARGINALIZED OPPOSITION

The Egyptian long history makes all analysts aware of the possibilities for Egyptian elite to enforce democracy. The courage of the revolutionary elite helped to hurry towards implementing democracy and human rights.

When Nasser came to power in 1954, he built the Socialist Arab Party (SAP). It was the unique party. Liberal, Islamist and communist parties were banned and their leaders arrested. During Anouar Sadat's period (1970–1981), pluralism was tolerated. That was in 1978. Many political parties were either reorganized or newly founded. Communists reappeared as the Work Party (WP). But shortly after, they made a strange coalition with Muslim Brothers, and they appoint them at the leadership of the party. Some of the WP intellectuals said that the coalition was a way to let people believe in communism. But what had happened was that communists not only believed in political Islamism, but they were totally annihilated. As the Work Party was considered an Islamist party, the government wanted in 2000 to ban it. Intellectuals who still believe in Nasserism built the Alarabi Nassery Party. Aluma (the nation) Party, Misr Alfath (openness of Egypt), the Greens, Social Justice, and Democratic People were small parties that made the Egyptian political scene more pluralistic and more diverse. New Wafd, and Alahrar came back with force, especially through their press. Some communists and nationalists formed the National Progressive Unionist Part (NPUP), and put at its head Khalid Muhi-eddin.

Although there were many pluralistic parliamentary elections, the New Wafd, Alahrar and The NPUP went on being marginalized groups that get very limited seats. When Husni Mubarak came to power, after Sadat was killed by the Islamist activist Alislambouli, he declared many times that the opposition is necessary to his regime, but the above mentioned parties did not gain ground. These parties say that falsification is the reason, but the government says that the results reflect the opposition's weight in society. In spite of being forbidden, some Islamist groups act on a wide range, and many times they do that violently. Many of their activists are jailed, and others are exiled. They call for *sharia* law. Deeply rooted in middle and poor classes, they contribute to social help for all those who are in need, and this makes them the most popular political fraction. Only Muslims are accepted to belong to the so called Islamist parties, and Copts who are the Christian minority in the country have no political representation, but some of its members belong to secular political parties.

Except for Muslim Brothers, who get 88 seats in 2006 parliamentary elections, all other political parties say that they are nationalists. Once claiming nationalism, it is agreed upon that democracy and human rights shouldn't count or it comes to the second position. The International

Institute for Democracy and Electoral Assistance (IDEA) says in a report titled "Democracy in the Arab World: Challenges, Achievements and Prospects" that there are "problems with indigenizing the concept of democracy. These problems have their roots in general illiteracy and extreme poverty, as well as in a lack of experience in democratic practice, structures and institutions. Violence, on the part of the government as well as certain groups, continues to be seen as a means to counter opposition, and thus further interferes with democratization" (20). The same institute notes that political parties are weak and cannot "play an effective role in politics and in building citizenship."

Liberals made huge steps at mid 2005 in expressing themselves. AL-Ghad party lead by Ayman Nour showed that liberals could put democracy forward in their struggle against the government.

CONCLUSION: INDIGENIZING DEMOCRACY

In NAC the elite is outside political parties. This elite would have played an important role in the democratization, or to what IDEA called "indigenizing the concept of democracy," especially for democratization as a whole which should start from the political parties themselves and spread all over the country. To attain this level, the educational system should educate about democracy, and building citizenship. The judiciary should be totally independent to be able to deal correctly with conflicts between the state and the political parties. Internal democracy, transparency and independence in decision-making are pre-conditions for the institutionalization of a functioning political party system. This may make limits to increasing fragmentations of parties, and participate in the reinforcement of the state, because in "a democracy [when] the legislature, the executive, and the party system act as independent parts [it reinforces] the larger political system" (1).

In NAC there is a great number of political groups acting outside the institution, especially the legislature. These groups represent themselves as an opposition to both the governments and their official opposition that acts from the inside legislature. This situation resulted in terrorist acts and harsh oppression. In Algeria, this reason led to real civil war. The same sit-

uation may threaten all other North African Countries if the official political system, including political parties and governments, goes on excluding
this outlawed opposition which may benefit from this situation to convince people about illegitimacy of governments, and corruption of recognized political parties. All official institutions should act to fulfill this task.
At the same time, if the radical opposition goes on to act outside institutions willingly, it will be annihilated. Extremism within the state in dealing with Islamist, and the Islamist parties' extremism in practice led to an
open confrontation between the two sides. Till now, there is no opportunity for reconciliation between the two parts. Each party considers the
other one betraying Islam and Muslims (2).

---

(1) International Institute for Democracy and Electoral Assistance.
Democracy in Deep-Rooted Conflict: Options for Negotiators, p222.
Harris, Peter and Ben Reilly (eds.), Stockholm, Sweden, 1998.
(2) The Muslim highly qualified scholars do not support Islamist extremism. The leaders of these movements are some political activists who take
Islam a veil to hide their political goal that is building a religious state
based on the one-party system.

VIII. Civil Society: Development, Transparency and Accountability

Civil society is a traditional phenomenon in NAC. It was a kind of non-institutionalized voluntary work. Without being organized, people used to associate with each other to serve the community. With colonization, both colonialists and liberation movements politicized this work. While the first wanted to destroy the values of indigenous people, the second wanted to cling to them and elaborate them more to be a nest for national activism. Political parties were not common, and ordinary people were not able to understand how to belong to them. Voluntary work was the medium to organize citizens in active movements against colonialism.

Volunteers turned easily to national activists through fighting the "outsiders." At the eve of countries' independence, nationalists were already rallied in political parties. As "civil society" is strongly related to "de-politicize" movements, in this too politicized situation, it was brought nearly to nil.

Shortly after the independence, the one-party regimes were in power, and all independent associations were outlawed. This made the civil society undergo a painful period. Also, where there was not a one-party system (Morocco for example), spaces of freedom were too narrow, and oppression was a common practice. Till 2005, the right to association had been abused with some differences from one country to another. Morocco is the only case where the right to build an association is less conditional. This right becomes final after receiving receipt for declaration to the administrative authority. No other agreement from the authorities is needed but sometimes they refuse to give the receipt. This simple act may make the founding outlawed. For the other North African Countries, any association should be authorized by the administrative authority to exercise its activities and this is a pre-condition for the association to be founded.

New pluralism brought with it some air to civil society. Before this, political activists who fled oppression and used it as a shade to their activities invaded it. With pluralism, it started to move towards de-politization. But movement is very slow especially that politicians wanted to use associations to their own political goals as lobbies to strengthen their positions in the political struggle. Though this situation is still obvious, civil society organizations (CSOs) had already started to influence the evolution of their countries.

Associations' work is a kind of voluntary service based on amateurism. This is due to lack of resources. Jobs cost much, and professionalism was not considered necessary to anything related to public interests, especially that the fields of action are limited to unpaid works and people refused to be paid and work full time for that. Actually, there is a transition towards professionalism especially when the association receives subsidies from the state. But this professionalism is itself drawn from amateurism, because professionals are not fully educated in administrating NGOs. This course is not taught at the universities. Only some international NGOs try from time to time to organize training seminars about capacity building, which had helped to the introduction of the beginning steps of professionalism.

Civil society in North African Countries is diverse. Associations, which do not work in a field related to politics, are freer than the others. Sometimes the right of association or freedom of activity may be abused, because the leader of the association or one of its influencing members has (or had) some political points of views that the government considers unacceptable. And if the field of action of the association is related in a way to politics, this is sufficient to put all the association members under scrutiny. If the association is related to the legal opposition, this is a reason for authorities to start a whole process of hesitation to offer all the legal rights to this "unwanted" newcomer. The situation starts to be very dangerous when the authorities consider that the association has some links with the outlawed opposition. Though the association does not state anything related to that in its status or in its background, its members are

harshly treated, and all their followers persecuted. Law enforcement officials treat NGOs according to their "intention" not action.

Freedom of association is related to political freedom in general. In
Morocco where opposition could come to power and govern and civil
society is freer, there are many problems related to authorities' practices. In
Libya there are no NGOs at all. The government grants the right of association to official institutions only. For Egypt the situation is totally different. In 1999, the parliament adopted a law that forces associations to
declare its resources and the same law forbid for any association to receive
foreign resources. Saâd Eddin Ibrahim the president of an association was
sentenced to ten years of imprisonment because he received subsidies for
his association from the United States of America. Although he is an
American citizen, he was judged for that because he also keeps the Egyptian citizenship and the law in this country does not recognize people's
rights to change the citizenship of birth. Due to international claims, Ibrahim was released afterwards.

Any feature of good governance cannot exist without a fully independent civil society in a democratic context. If civil society is sometimes
independent towards governments, it is not so towards political parties
and political groups. It goes on serving as a shade to all oppressed activities.

UNDP, USAID, and some French and German cooperation bodies
and NGOs try through their civil society program to help NGOs to
develop themselves and acquire self-initiation, good administration, and
an accountably system. In its thesis about sustainable human development, UNDP says that its facilitating capability is related to:

> "1. Encouraging and enabling active involvement of the right mix of
> actors;
>
> 2. Allowing and promoting a free exchange of information and ideas
> up; and down stream as well as horizontally between government
> departments and civil society organizations (CSOs); and
>
> 3. Institutionalizing more participatory approaches to self human
> development, which engage CSOs.

Foreign bodies cannot substitute the role of governments and civil society itself to promote its activities. But they can help by their experience and methods and views. Sometimes they may help by funding CSOs activities, which had helped civil society to be stronger. This empowerment should take into consideration that many CSOs are used for private goals, or for the account of extremist political groups.

CSO should be a watchdog not an active political section. Its role is to safeguard values of democracy, transparency, and voluntary service. It may struggle for fair and free elections, but its credibility lays in not participating in it. The opposite means that it might be a government formed by civil society organizations. At that time there would be no civil society at all because it should govern and if it looses elections it will turn to the opposition. However its form of organization is the opposition is not a part of the civil society.

In North African Countries, civil society is one of the major factors that may guarantee stability in the country, especially with political tensions, and ethnic based political groups as it is for the Algerian case.

With the weakness of the political parties, civil society may lead the struggle for democracy, especially if it succeeds in protecting its independence from both the government and the political parties. Till now the most active NGOs (CSOs) are those specialized in human rights. They consider democracy a *sine qua nun* condition to the state of law. Also, they think that development, transparency, and accountability added to democracy, lead to a prosperous society.

Since their independence North African Countries have been saying that their aim is to build their countries economy after decades of colonialism. The latest (Algeria) got its independence in 1962, till 2005 they all are still underdeveloped. Once a government is not elected, automatically it is not accountable towards the people. This helps its members to act as they see fit without any fear of being asked questions about its action. When a government is not accountable, how it can be transparent? Transparency means equality between different economic actors, acting according to appropriate management procedures, and to work for the public good. In recent years, civil society was invested in development projects, promotion of education, and the struggle against corruption.

Corruption is one of the major handicaps to development in North African Countries. It involves unlawful enrichment, and misuse of power. This results in the total destruction of the economy. Although laws are severe, they are not applicable on the ground. The situation differs from one country to another, but generally governments ignore bribes takers. Sure, there is the need for new laws and institutions to fight against corruption and make state officials accountable, but when existing laws are not enforced, adding new laws will be like a farce. Transparency International fights in the whole region, especially in Morocco, where it has its section, against corruption. Campaigns are launched, and propositions to amend laws are made.

Women organizations still face huge problems. Obscurantist movements led harsh campaigns against their members, and try to force governments to ban their activities. But North African women showed courage, strength, and wit that had hindered all their opponents' activities. New ways to struggle against discrimination are on the way, especially by the creation of training centers for women to fight for their rights and to help themselves to gain their living to be more independent towards the man. In the pure and general political struggle, women's rights may be lost. But promoting economic and cultural conditions of women and pushing them to acquire self-confidence are the most important tools that help them to fight for their rights.

Organizations for child's rights, environments, handicaps etc...are numerous and their activities are diverse.

Also, a clear independence from the political parties and governments is a condition for them to be more strong and influential. Through this independence, they may help both the governments and the opposition.

PART IV

IX. Conclusion:
The Zero Stage of States

In modern times, the majority of states are based on democratic elections and the rule of law. Once a law is adopted, its enforcement becomes automatic. The violation of these laws may be committed, but the courts are obliged and expected to punish violators. I think that democratic elections, a fair judiciary and a transparent economic system are the minimum standards any state should keep. Otherwise, it is considered a "negative state". The "positive state" embodies more elements than those mentioned.

To achieve more than the minimum is related to the implementation of political and economic reforms, which may be proposed by political parties and implemented by the democratically elected governments. These reforms are launched after the programs having been voted for in elections and adopted by the legislative institutions. Reforms need devoted leaders for their implementation in practice and flexible mechanisms to assure their execution. Accountability will help to assure integrity of civil servants and private sector employees. Total devotion is required to promote common values to make them based on human rights and the common interest, which in turn serve as the keystone for development. But if there is a "negative state", there is no possibility to see these things taking place. Where we find the "negative state", there is authoritarianism, illiteracy, underdevelopment and poverty.

The governments in the "positive states" are accountable periodically before voters. Since the day of declaring the results of elections, the political parties start to think about the next campaign. So, they are obliged to meet peoples' needs. If not, they may fail in the subsequent elections. If a civil servant takes bribes, he will be charged, tried and punished. Judges decide according to laws. In the similar conditions all those who are paid by the state become real civil servants.

Between the "positive state" and the "negative state" there is the "zero state", which is the adequate state for the minimum standards of the state. At "0" level, the whole framework of the state should be able to execute development programs that may be launched. The "zero state" level is a pre-condition for the implementation of good governance principles.

In recent centuries, the state used to have different forms and aims. Since the 18th century as we had seen before, political leaders started to consider "people's sovereignty" and also right to security, freedom from arbitrary arrest and at least a minimal standard of welfare. During these periods, this was the higher maximum how a modern state should be.

Today at the beginning of the third millennium, to guarantee the democratic sovereignty should be the lowest minimum. It is the stage "0" of the state. Regional and international organizations try to determine how people's sovereignty should be protected. The General Assembly of the United Nations had adopted many instruments about democracy such as the International Covenant on Civil and Political Rights (hereinafter the Covenant), which protects the right of every citizen to take part in the conduct of public affairs, the right to vote and be elected and have the right to have access to public service (article 25). In the general comments to this article adopted by the Committee on Civil and Political Rights at its 1510th meeting (fifty seventh session) on 12 July 1996, it was made clear that "whatever form of constitution or government is in force, the Covenant requires States to adopt such legislative and other measures as may be necessary to ensure that citizens have an effective opportunity to enjoy the rights it protects."

A democratic government should be based on the consent of people. The legislative institutions, which should have full right to oversight the executive and make legislation, have be freely and fairly elected. Also, the citizens' right to change the constitution should be protected without any distinction between them on the grounds of race, color, sex, language, religion, political or other opinion, national or social origin, property, birth or any other status.

The first text approved in the United Nations that recognized explicitly the existence of a right to democracy is resolution 1999/57, of 27 April 1999, which was on the promotion of the right to democracy. Adopted by 51 votes to none, this resolution affirmed that the right to democratic governance include, *inter alia*, the following: a) The right to freedom of expression, association and believe; b) The rule of law, fairness in the administration of justice and independence of the judiciary; c) the right of citizens to choose their governmental system through constitutional or other democratic means; d) the right of political participation, including equal opportunity for citizens to become candidates; d) Transparent and accountable government institutions (N. E/CN.4/RES/1999/57, 28 April 1999, Paragraph 2.)

At Its fifty-second session, the Sub-Commission on the Promotion and Protection of Human Rights approved resolution 2000/116 entrusting the UN expert Manuel Rodriguez Cuadros to prepare a working paper on the measures provided in the various international human rights instruments for the promotion and consolidation of democracy. M. R. Cuadros wrote in his paper that democracy is "a value under international protection." His reference is the above mentioned resolution 1999/57 of the Commission on Human Rights that declared the commission "resolved, on the eve of a new century and millennium, to take all measures within its power to secure for all people the fundamental democratic rights and freedoms." Considering the rule of law, Cuadros says that it is reflected in the "legal relation between the State with the enjoyment of fundamental rights and on the exercise by the State of the duty to guarantee." He adds that the rule of law requires at least three limitations on State authority: a material limitation, related to the respect for and guarantee of fundamental freedoms and human rights; a functional limitation, in the form of a division of powers; and a temporal limitation, expressed as the periodic renewal of the people's will through free and fair elections.

The Universal Declaration of Human Rights had already established a link between the rule of law and democracy when it stated in article 21 that: "The will of the people shall be the basis of the authority of government; this will shall be expressed in periodic and genuine elections which shall be by universal and equal suffrage and shall be held by secret vote or by equivalent free voting procedure." It is obvious that the Declaration did not state openly that there is a right to democracy. More than this it talks about "secret vote or…" as if there is the possibility to have a vote which is not secret but in which the will of people will be respected. The will of the people underwent a number of revisions in the Commission of Human Rights in June 1948. The United Kingdom advanced a shorter version not containing any references to the will of the people as the basis of the authority of government, to elections, or to equal access to public service. The United Kingdom "desired a shorter and more general text in part because of its concern with the application of political rights in colonies" (see Allan Rosas, Article 21, in "The Universal Declaration of Human Rights—A Common Standard of Achievement, pp 431-451).

The Council of Europe had adopted the "European Charter of Local Self-Government" in 1985. In the Preamble it is stated that the "right of citizens to participate in the conduct of public affairs is one of the democratic principles that are shared by all member States of the Council of Europe." This convention is legally binding to member states. Its second article provides that: "the principle of local self-government shall be recognized in domestic legislation, and where practicable in the constitution." The Inter-American Convention on human Rights (article23), and the Constitutive Act of the African Union (the Preamble) refer to democracy and respect of people's will. These regional instruments of human rights that govern the majority of states in Europe, the Americas and Africa represent a medium to enforce democracy and the rule of law.

The United Nations had created in 1994, the Electoral Assistance Division within the Department of Political Affairs. It is in charge of monitoring elections all over the world. But it is not the lonely department that deals with electoral matters. The UNDP, the Department of Economic and Social Affairs, the Office for Project Services and the United Nations High Commissioner for Human Rights intervene in the promotion of democracy and the respect of citizens will. In his report "In larger freedom: towards development, security and human rights for all" (2005) the Secretary-General of the United Nations Kofi Anan declared that "the right to choose how to be ruled, and how rules them must be the birthright of all people."

With all the instruments and the mechanisms mentioned above, the international community is able to enforce the minimum standards of the state. It is possible to have "Zero stage of states" all over the globe. At that time, humanity may start thinking about "positive states", but as the "negative state" is a common phenomenon in many regions of the world, the struggle for democracy, the rule of law, transparency, and the independence of justice seem still too long.

What is the case for North African Countries?

In North African Countries, governments are not drawn from free and fair elections. The mechanisms of the implementation of the rules adopted by the legislative institutions are not efficacious. Many components of the opposition are banned. Freedom of association and expression is not protected. Ethnic tensions and political extremism are gaining ground. The military is an influential political apparatus that supports governments. Justice is unfair and its bodies are weak. Banking systems are not transparent. Corruption, an unaccountable puffed up administration and family based private sector jeopardize the economic activity. Human rights are not protected and there are systematic violations. Women are marginalized. Children are exploited against their right to natural growth. Poverty and want threaten to destruct the structures of society that protect moral values. These are some results of the governance described along the previous chapters. There is a gap between law and practice. Some basic laws including constitutions are against democratic principles and human rights' international conventions. People are still not used enough to act according to laws. They have the habit of acting according to their local cultural values and the common traditions. The adopted laws are not made known among peoples. There are high rates of illiteracy and governments do not make any efforts to explain to their citizens which laws govern them. Neither the television nor the radio is used as a medium for that.

In North African Countries, the state is a new apparatus. The tribal habits influence the state's behavior. The brother-in-law of the president is a prominent person in the state. In fact, he enjoys from impunity. People from the same tribe are privileged. This is a common practice for both high and low state officials. Leaders used to profit from the popular support as national unaccountable leaders more than public servants. There are some political parties based on ethnic and religious ideologies. In a similar atmosphere, it is not easy to establish a democratic state. In spite of this, there is an emerging democratic society represented especially by the diversity of political ideas, multi-party system and the growing opposition. The state is still the "negative state." It is far of reaching the zero stage of the state. To attain this level they have to perform structural reforms such as:

1. **Bridging the gap between law and practice:** This is the most difficult task in North Africa where traditional unwritten laws had been governing the population for centuries. Most of the illiterate people believe in Islam and say prayers without being able to read or understand any verse of the Koran. The same goes for the rights and duties of citizenship. All what most people know about their country is its name. Sometimes, there are those who do not know the name of the president of the state. Laws are enacted within the elite, but not within common people. To bridge the gap between laws and practice may be carried into effect as a result of promoting education in all its forms and of the county's economic development. These laws before and after being adopted by the legislative institutions have to be explained by the mass-medias including the radio and the television. The laws should be explained on a large scale to citizens wherever they are: in big cities or small towns. This kind of projects shall involve the state, political parties and the civil society. The law is a result of a specific culture in specific conditions. So, before changing laws, it is needed to change people's mind. Once a law is emanating from people or at least the majority, it will be not only integrated in their practices, but protect by them.

2. **Multi-party system and political bi-polarity within the same society:** As it was explained earlier, the multi-party system is a new phenomenon in the region. In Morocco, despite the fact that the 1962's constitution declares that the one-party system is forbidden, the opposition enjoyed of a limited freedom. It was prosecuted and its leaders arrested. In all other North African countries, there was no lawful opposition at all. The one-party system was enforced and all other political parties were banned. Unfortunately, the regimes were supported by he people because of some decisions that they were taken in favor of the population, such as agricultural reforms, which provided that some parcels of land were distributed to small farmers, but it was proved that these kinds of projects were not successful. To develop agricultural production, you need not these parcels, but large farms. Since the end of the eighties, except Libya, all North African countries banned the one-party system in hurried and unprepared constitutional reforms. Of course, the right of association should be protected anywhere and always. But to establish the multi-party system after decades of totalitarianism and without any transitional steps, a high probability of chaos cannot be avoided. Under such condition, education for democracy is particularly indispensable. The first wave of the new political parties, especially in Algeria, Tunisia and Egypt, brought strong Islamist movements who tried to enforce *sharia* law (Islamic law). Islamists were the strong and most credible opposition in all North African countries. The lack of democratic elections brought about the demise of political parties. These parties became like the corrupted administration and gathered around them thousands of opportunists whose aim is only to profit from privileges. The governing parties have been in power for many years, which means that they had no opportunity to go to opposition and renew their elite and ideas at the same time. In every country, there are at least six major political parties. Each one presents its candidates to the elections independently from the others. The result is that all the parties find themselves

weak and cannot face the party in power. A coalition would have
been the mean to gather all forces and try to win elections to form
the cabinet. This experience was tried in Morocco where King
Hassan II had called the ex-opposition to form the cabinet as it
was mentioned before. The ex-governing parties went to the
opposition, but they could not cope as they had governed for very
long periods, some of them had spent in power about 20 years.
Instead of restoring their positions with people, these old parties
became meaningless and Islamists had strengthened their positions. Multi-party system and political bipolarity within the same
society are the keys to enforce democracy and to make the state's
image respected among its citizens.

3. **Promoting Human rights:** Respect of human dignity in its natural form is a traditional practice in North African culture. Islam
   urges believers to respect human beings whatever his religion, age,
   or sex are. At the same time, leading common life makes the right
   to private life or personal positions less protected than what is provided by laws because of the gap mentioned above. There is the
   need for national programs on education to human rights in
   schools and through the mass media. All north African countries
   signed and ratified the major international conventions, such as
   the Covenant on Civil and Political Rights, The covenant on Economic, Social and cultural Rights, the Convention Against Torture, and the Convention of the Elimination of All sorts of
   Discrimination against Women. All they need is to enforce these
   conventions and some others through their legislation and dissem-
   inate them within the population. Human rights' NGOs should
   be tolerated and sustained, political prisoners released, and the
   press freed.

4. **Independence of Justice:** In North African countries, laws guarantee the independence of the judiciary, but as law enforcement
   officials are not educated enough for the independence of justice
   and most of the judges are easy to corrupt because of their low

moral standards. To promote the independence of justice, it is necessary to promote respect for human rights and integrity among all people related to the system of justice through long-term programs. Large investments should be made in recruiting human resources, especially that there are very few judges in comparison to the numbers required. One judge may decide on one hundred cases per day. Openness to the international experience would be helpful. Most of the judges had not the opportunity to learn about the European and American judicial systems. More than this, most of them do not speak any foreign language.

5. **Legislative strengthening:** Where they really exist, parliaments are still far of implementing their roles as people's representatives. The political systems need a reengineering to enforce balance of powers and accountability. This is a strategic project to democratize the region and empower citizens and make them able to make change whenever and wherever it's needed. Constitutional and institutional reforms to make parliamentarians able to decide are determinant for the any democracy. Rubberstamp parliaments are useless.

6. **Transparency:** Transparency should be practiced not only in the political field, but also in the economic one. First of all, the structures and functions of the government, public sector and private sector should be clearly defined. Government involvement in the private sector should be conducted in an open and public manner, and on the basis of clear rules and procedures that are applied in a nondiscriminatory way. A clear legal and administrative framework for fiscal management is needed. Comprehensive budget laws and openly available administrative rules should govern any commitment or expenditure of public funds. Taxes, duties, fees and charges should have an explicit legal basis. Ethical standards of behavior for public servants should be clear and well publicized. Full information about economic activity of governments should be provided. Corruption should be punished, but before that,

wide campaigns explaining laws and people's economic rights should be launched. Transparency leads to an economic system based on the open competition.

7. **Development:** Development is a combination of numerous factors: democracy, good head for business, flexibility of economic laws and the will of the nation as a whole. It cannot be achieved in one day. It is a long-term project to which the state should dedicate a lot of its resources. The development hoped for through the socialist systems in Algeria, Libya and Egypt had vanished and left behind totally corrupted economies. Moroccan and Tunisian hopes for development were not clearly defined. These two countries were permanently preoccupied by their internal stability more than anything else. I do not think that there is a prescription about how development should be made, but the mentioned principles should be helpful.

8. **Civil Society:** If the press is the fourth power, we can say that the civil society is the fifth. It influences the public opinion and force governments to take or draw some of its positions. Nearly like the parliament, its role is obvious in modern societies. In North African countries, NGOs should be more vigorous. Their strength would be based on professionalism and getting rid of taking political positions or being affiliated to political parties. The civil society's relation with the state is either a total opposition or a complete dependence. This is not how the civil society should be. It should work with the state in partnership with keeping its independence in the decision-making. Islamic organizations investment in politics was a handicap more than an advantage to build a democratic society. They would have invested themselves in the civil society like some Christian movements that were devoted to the defense of religious values instead of defending political pragmatic positions. There are many other Islamic organizations that refuse to be involved in political activities and go on working in education and sustaining the poor. But at the beginning of the

new century, they represent a minority if compared to those with political tendencies.

9. **Regional Cooperation:** North African countries are on the southern coast of the Mediterranean. To the north there is the European Union. The cooperation between the two sides would have been more effective if there were a union to the south of the northern one. Recently a principle agreement was signed by North African Countries to establish a free economic zone along the Mediterranean coast. It is an important step that should be developed to a real agreement. In 2001, borders were closed between Morocco and Algeria and between Libya and Tunisia. Most of the exchange rates are between each country and the European counties or the European Union as a whole. To draw investments to the region, governments are obliged to open borders and keep similar rules for the market and try to think about establishing a single currency. There is the Maghrib Arab Union, but includes Mauritania and excludes Egypt. The Arab Union is a farce that had ended before the curtain rises. A North African Union would be a strategic alliance between countries of similar history, religion and culture. Identical problems are also helpful for these states to be united. The unification of laws to the larger possible extent, as it is the case for the northern European countries (Denmark, Sweden and Finland), would make the union real. It is not necessary to unite all laws, but those that influence democracy, investments and human rights should protect common values and be based on united principles. The most crucial idea is democracy. The will of the people should be the origin to form a cabinet. This is not something difficult to reach an agreement about it. Huge problems may rise only if this proposition was suggested by any state.

In November 1995, the European Union countries and their counterparts from 12 Mediterranean countries signed an agreement upon the progressive establishment of a vast Euro—Mediterranean free trade area, to be completed by 2010. More than free trade, those who signed Barcelona agreement were aiming to promote democracy, stability and peace in the Mediterranean area through a reinforcement of political dialogue and security. Also, another major goals was to deepen rapprochement between peoples through a social and human partnership. This agreement was a real challenge for North African countries. It had opened opportunities and dangers. After six years, dangers are still facing the North African economy and opportunities are not used. North African countries did not use the principal financial instrument of the European Union for the implementation of the Euro—Mediterranean partnership called MEDA. The program offers technical and financial support measures to accompany the reform of economic and social structures for the Mediterranean partners. This program supports economic transition and aims to prepare for the implementation of free trade through increasing competitiveness with a view to achieving sustainable economic growth, strengthening the socio-economic balance. This is the most important opportunity opened by Barcelona process, but dangers may be summarized in the economic disability of North African countries to be competitive towards the states of the European Union.

With all the eight conditions above and may be more, the North African countries may reach the stage of "state 0". These conditions may seem senseless to any citizen of the Western European or North American counties, but calling for these things in North Africa still costs prison sentences, exile, torture and killings

The political will expressed by the king of Morocco and some other presidents let the hope possible for a democratic North Africa as a condition for development and the establishment of "the positive states". But there are not only kings and presidents that decide for the fate of their countries. The states' institutions and elites still not aware about the danger the "negatives states" represent for the present, the future or may be the past also.

The traditional understanding of governance of the majority of the people in North Africa should be overturned as governance has been re-conceptualized and its new meaning that was adopted by many international institutions has nothing to do with the political and economic situation, which North Africans endure.

Bibliography

Books and Articles

ROGER SCRUTON. <u>Dictionary of Political Thought</u>. Second edition. MACMILLAN. 1996.

AIN MCLEAN. <u>Oxford Concise Dictionary of Politics</u>. Oxford University Press. 1996.

Cassier. <u>The Myth of State</u>. London. 1946.

Niccolo Machiavelli, Te Prince (Le Prince).

Christine Fame. <u>Les Declarations Des Droits de l''Homme de 1789"</u> <u>(1789's Human Rights declarations)</u>. Petite Payot. 1998.

Gregory H. Fox and Brad R. Roth. <u>Democratic Governance and International Law (Introduction: The Spread of Liberal Democracy).</u> Cambridge University Press. 2000.

Burdeau (George). <u>L'ETAT (The State).</u>

UNDP. <u>Re-conceptualizing Governance</u>—Discussion paper 1, New York, January 1977.

UNDP<u>. Re-conceptualizing Governance</u>—Discussion paper 2, New York, January 1977.

UNDP. <u>Re-conceptualizing Governance</u>—Discussion paper 3, New York, January 1977.

Montesquieu. <u>DE L'ESPRIT DES LOIS"—Book I.</u>

Montesquieu. <u>DE L'ESPRIT DES LOIS"—Book II.</u>

Abdessalam Yassine. Enlightenment of women (Tanouir Almouminat). Afak imp. Casablanca: 1997.

Humbaraci (Arslan). Algeria: A Revolution that failed, A political History since 1954. New York: Praeger. 1966.

Habib Souaidia. The Dirty War (La Salle Guerre). Edition la Decouverte. Paris: 2001.

Camille et Yves Lacoste. L'Etat du Maghrib, ed le Fennec. Casablanca: 1997.

Hopwood (Derek). Egypt: Politics and Society, 1945–1984. Boston: Allen and Unwin. 1985.

McDermott (Anthony). Egypt from Nasser to Mubarak: A flawd Revolution. London: Croom Helm. 1988.

Deeb, Marius. Party politics in Egypt: the Wafd and Its Rivals, 1919–1939. London: State University of New York Press. 1971.

Benjamin (Stora). Voies Singulieres pour Allier Islam et Modernite (Unique Ways to Rally Islam to Modernity). Paris: De l'Atelier. 1999.

"Islam, Democracy, and the State: The Reemergence of Authoritarian Politics in Algeria." Paper presented at 18th Annual Symposium. Center for Contemporary Arab Studies. Georgetown University on "Islam and Secularism in North Africa." Washington: April 1–2, 1993.

William Zartman. "Algeria: Technocratic Rule, Military Power", In Political elite in Arab north Africa: Morocco, Algeria, Tunisia, Libya, and Egypt. New York: Longman. 1982.

"Algeria under Chadli: Liberalization Without Democratisation or Prestoroika, Yes; Glasnost, No." In Middle East Insight, 6, No.3. 1988.

Ottawa, David B. and Marina Ottaway. Algeria: The Politics of socialist revolution. Berkely: University of California Press. 1970.

Boukhobza, Mohamed. <u>Reptures et Transformations Sociales en Algerie</u> <u>(The Cut and Social Transformation in Algeria)</u>. Algiers: office des publications universities. 1989.

Hunter, Robert. <u>Egypt under the Khedives, 1805–1879: From Household Government to Modern Bureaucracy</u>. Pittsburg: University pf Pittsburgh. 1984.

Hopwood, Derek. <u>Egypt: Politics and society, 1945–1984.</u> Boston. Allen and Unwin, 1985.

Ibrahim, Ibrahim<u>. Religion and politics under Nasser and sadat, 1952–1981</u>. In Barbara Freyer stowasser (ed.9 The Islamic Impulse (pp 121-134), London: croom Helm, 1987.

Mcdermott, Anthony. <u>Egypt from Nasser to Mubarak: A Flawed Revolution</u>. London: Croom Helm. 1988.

Vatikiotis, P.J. <u>The History of Egypt from Muhammad Ali to Sadat.</u> Baltimore: Johns Hopkings university Press. 1980.

Saab, Gabriel. <u>The Egyptian Agrarian Reform, 1952–1962.</u> London: Oxford university Press. 1967.

Dekmejian, Richard Hrair. <u>Egypt Under Nasir: A study in Political dynamics.</u> Albany: State University of New York Press, 1971.

Harik, Iliya. <u>Continuity and change in Local Development policies in Egypt</u>. In International Journal of Middle east studies, 16, No.1, 1984.

Gudmander Alfredsson, and Asbjorn Eide. <u>The Universal Declaration of Human Rights—A common Standard of Achievement.</u> The Hague: Martinus Nijhoff Publishers. 2000.

United Nations. Human Rights—<u>A compilation of International Instruments—Volume 1 (First part) Universal Instruments.</u> New York and Geneva. 1996.

United Nations. Human Rights—<u>A compilation of International Instru-ments—Volume 1 (Second part) Universal Instruments.</u> New York and Geneva. 1996.

Ellen Alderman, and Caroline Kennedy. <u>Pour Notre Defence—La Decla-ration des Droits Americaine au Quotidien.</u> Nancy: Presses Universitaires de Nancy. 1991.

IDEA. <u>Democracy in the Arab World.</u> Stockholm, Sweden. 2000.

T.P. VAN REENEN. <u>The Right to Development in International And Municipal Law.</u> In The African Society of International and Comparative law. Seventh Annual Conference. Johannesburg. 21–24 August 1995.

<u>Yearbook of Islamic and Middle Eastern Law.</u> Volume 4. General Edi-tions: Eugene Cortan, and Chibli Mallat. Kluwer law International. 1997–1998.

Ursula A. O'Hare. <u>Realizing Human Rights for Women</u>. Human Rights Quarterly. Volume 21. Number 1. February 1999.

Abdullahi Ahmed An-Nai'm. <u>Human Rights In Muslim world: Socio-Political Conditions and Scriptural Imperatives.</u> In Harvard Human Rights Journal. Volume 3. Spring 1990.

References: Web Sites and Documents on the net:

Constitutions of Morocco, Algeria, Tunisia, Libya, and Egypt. (<u>www.urisch.edu/~jpjones/confinder/const.htm</u>).

Country Studies: Congress Library.

County Studies: IMF

World reports: The World Bank

World Reports 2000/2001: Amnesty International, Human Rights Watch, and Federation International des Doits De l'Homme.

Freedom House Report.

Transparency International web site: www.transparency.org

Countries Web Sites:

Morocco: www.mincom.gov.ma
        www.maec.gov.ma

Algeria: www.arabia.com/algeria
        (opposition) www.hms-algeria.net

Tunisia: www.ministeres.tn

Libya: www.mathaba.net/info

Egypt: www.sis.gov.eg/

NGOs web sites:

http://www.civicus.org

National Democratic Institute. "Political Overview. http://www.ndi.org (see also, worldwide activities).

Country Reports and committees observations:
UNHCHR: www.unhchr.ch/

978-0-595-40898-6
0-595-40898-2

www.ingramcontent.com/pod-product-compliance
Lightning Source LLC
Chambersburg PA
CBHW020412290526
45785CB00002B/532